Emotional Intelligence

a Practical Guide

By: Jackson A. Thomas - Debbie Lancer

Table of Contents

Introduction

According to Daniel Goleman, a popular book writer ion 1996, emotional intelligence is the ability to understand, recognize, and manage our emotions. Goleman also believes that it is the ability to understand and influence others' emotions as well.

These things that emotional intelligence describes are important in the workplace, at home, and through life. These traits and behaviors help you to live a life that you will better understand and enjoy. Too many people in today's society are falling too short of common sense, and social capabilities. Whether it stems from a lack of parental influence or a lack of involvement with other children in the younger stages of life, people today are becoming less aware of how we should act and think in our everyday lives and instead rely on their emotions to quickly influence their words and behaviors.

Science has stated that in almost every society of the world, we have all began to get dumber. An example of studies showing a decline in intelligence can be seen by Norway's Ragnar Frisch Centre for Economic Research and the work they have done regarding the intelligence of Norwegian men. The center analyzed nearly 730,000 IQ tests given to Norwegian men before their compulsory military service from 1970 to 2009, and they found that average IQ scores were becoming steadily lower. It was not by any small or meaningless amount either. With each generation of Norwegian men, there seemed to be a drop in 7 IQ points on average.

In another study, the National Academy of the Sciences of the United States of America examined the IQ scores of men born between 1962 and 1991. Researchers found that scores increased for men born between 1962 and 1975. However, among men born after 1975, they steadily decreased.

Why do you think this is? Why would you guess that people are progressively dumbing down? Maybe this is a problem directly related to genetics. This could be the result of the hypothesis made popular by the movie "Idiocracy", and that dumb people have more children. Or perhaps it was only the group of genetics within the groups studied. The hypothesis states that since it is more commonly the uneducated people who have larger families, and the more educated people tend to think carefully about their family planning process, the dumber genetics are being passed down too quickly for the more intelligent genetics to catch up. This is like imagining a hillbilly family with no education living in the mountains with 6 children in every generation, while the scientist and his wife decide to have only one child because each of them are so busy.

We can assume that this has a part in the decline of intelligence, but we may also look to nurture rather than nature for the answer. The times have changed, and perhaps our modern environment requires less knowledge. Everything in today's society is about pleasure, easy access, and convenience. Today, almost every person on the street has a cellphone. Smartphones and smart devices do almost everything for us. They can order food for us, hail a cab, find someone to walk your dog, do your taxes, and even shop for you. We simply do not use our brains as much as we used to, and only a fool would deny it.

Perhaps we could blame it on the media. The media has become increasingly trashy and glorifies people who are uneducated. Think about what is popular in today's music and think about the people making the music. The music is written mostly in slang and glorifies the incorrect pronunciations of many words and phrases. For example, listen to Kanye West's "Jesus Walks". In this song, Kanye sings,"We at war with terrorism, racism, and most of all, we at war with ourselves. God, show me the way because the Devil trying to break me down." It is easy to see the grammar mishaps in this phrase, and when compared to music years ago, it really isn't much different. The big difference is the level at which this type of communication language is accepted. Today, modern music hardly uses real instruments when compared to 50 years ago. The creation of auto-tune went viral and caused a massive decline in the need for musicians who play real instruments.

It is also highly arguable that this may be due to the schooling system being far less than adequate in some of the world's largest countries. The United States, in particular, has seen a large decline in the quality of our schooling. Arne Duncan, who has spent his entire life in and around the school system, writes in his book that **"our educational system is essentially built to create assembly line workers and that**

the system is exceptionally ill-prepared to meet the needs of today's students."

Arne goes further to discuss how the American school system has not made almost any changes whatsoever to adjust to the educational needs of our children in nearly 100 years. He writes that we are being out-educated, out-invested, and out-innovated by other countries. We are no longer competing for jobs and opportunities amongst ourselves on a state vs. state level, but we are now competing with China and India and the U.K. for these things. We are competing with them even within our own country with the increase of students traveling abroad for a college education. When a student travels abroad to the United States to compete for a slot in a university or company, often they are coming because even they are very aware that they are more prepared education-wise for these positions.

Arne states further that he believes the cause of the failing school systems in the United States are being caused by a total lack of political will to make positive change. The number of politicians who are willing to make a change for our kids is few. America just does not value teaching as much as it used to.

The bottom line to all of this is we do not know what is causing the recent decline in intelligence, but by understanding emotional intelligence and creating a better modern society, we can make the world a better place. Through care and hard work, we can educate ourselves to a higher standard than what may or may not have been set for us by our parents, legislature, and government. The culture of easy access and convenience will more than likely stay, as it is human nature to seek things that are pleasurable and easy, but we can make ourselves into better people, and highly functioning members of this world.

Chapter 1: What is Emotional Intelligence?

According to the dictionary, emotional intelligence is *the capacity to be aware of, control, and express one's emotions, and to handle interpersonal relationships judiciously and empathetically.*

One's emotional intelligence, or EQ, is often compared to one's IQ. There are five categories to your EQ.

1. Self regulation - Often when you feel your emotions, you can not or have little of control for them. It is difficult to control when you feel a certain way, or how intense your feelings are, and it is also difficult to stop yourself from reacting negatively when you feel this way. Even though these things are true, there are a number of ways you may decrease the amount of time these emotions exist. These techniques also alleviate the negative emotions you feel such as anger, sadness, jealousy, and frustration. One technique is rethinking the situation which led to these emotions and seeing it in a different perspective. By positively thinking, you can see your situation in perhaps a brighter light. Instead of worrying about how there was a hair in your food, maybe instead choose to recognize that you got a free meal today. Other techniques include breathing exercises, taking a walk, or self meditation.

2. Self awareness- Being self aware allows one to recognize when they are feeling a negative emotion as it happens. A person who practices self-awareness is able to put aside what their body is

telling them to do in response to a negative emotion and think before they react. The two major elements of self-awareness are self confidence and emotional awareness. When you are self-aware, it will be easier for you to understand others and then detect how they think of you. Another Pro to practicing awareness is opening a new opportunity for change within your life. As you develop your awareness, your thought processes and behaviors will change. You will recognize where these negative feelings are leading you and you will learn to make the necessary changes.

3. Motivation- Motivation requires goal-setting and a clear mind. You must be able to focus on what you want and see that you can reach it.Motivation also circle back to self-confidence and positive thinking. You will quickly lose motivation when you feel as if you are failing too often or not moving quick enough. Instead of seeing a failure, it would best benefit you to see an opportunity to learn and try again. There are four major components of motivation: achievement drive, commitment, initiative, and optimism.

4. Empathy- Being able to detect how the people who surround you feel is important in daily living. Humans are social animals and require interaction. When you no longer practice empathy, you lose friends.

5. Social Skills- By the overuse of technology by people in 2019, we have lost our ability to use "people skills". Because of this, our interpersonal skills have not been present in the workplace

or at home. Social skills are the skills you have which help you interact with people everyday.

When people with high EQ and IQ succeed, there are several factors contributing to their success. Scientists have agreed the your IQ accounts for roughly 10% of your successes, and the rest depends on your EQ among other things. Some signs of having a higher than normal EQ are as follows.

You are able to pause in conversation. This shows that you are stopping and thinking before saying anything further. This is restraining you from making a permanent decision influenced by an emotion that is not permanent, but only temporary. Someone who considers their words considers themselves and that is a direct demonstration of self-awareness.

You show that you are authentic. This does not mean that you are oversharing everything about yourself, but rather you are showing everyone that you are friendly and approachable. You say what you mean without being skippy about the details. You are sure of yourself because you know that even if people don't appreciate what you say and do, the ones who matter will.

You consciously attempt to control your thoughts and behaviors. It is very difficult to control your emotions, but it is not that difficult to control how you react to them. No one wants to be a slave to their emotions, and you can overcome the primal urge to throw a lamp across the room when you are angry.

You consider the feeling of others.People who have a high EQ are not only self-aware, but they also have a high level of social awareness. When you are able to be aware of those around you, you will be able to properly gauge the audience. You will be able to answer questions regarding your social weaknesses and social strengths, how your current mood is affecting your thoughts and feelings, and what you are feeling beneath the surface of what you show others.

You are not only able to be challenged with questioned, but you actually apply and accept constructive criticism. Negative feedback is never an enjoyable thing to be given, but it shows good character in someone who can first think before responding and actually gain from it. I am not only referencing criticism that is kind, but the criticism that is rudely given or poorly delivered as well.

You frequently praise others. Being able to tell someone at work that they did a good job really allows you to grow as a person. Sometimes we get caught within our failures and it feels like we do not want to see others succeeding. Being supportive of each other, however, makes the world a better place. You will build trust by giving your fellows the acknowledgement and credit that they deserve, and you will inspire them to be the best version of themselves.

You are able to recognize your mistakes and apologize. Apologizing takes a lot of character. Demonstrating humility shows others that you are authentic and intelligent, and a truly intelligent person has no problem admitting when they are wrong. Emotional intelligence shows you that when you give an apology, it isn't always because you were wrong, but it can be given because you value your friendship with someone.

Emotionally Intelligent people keep their promises and help others. A promise is sacred and intelligent people know that when you break a promise, you damage your trust. It not only damages relationships, but your name is damaged as well, and people will no longer want to trust you. Also, being trustworthy is a big part of being able to help others, too. Helping others is easier to do when people want to trust you with their things and their tasks.

Emotional Intelligence is an easy concept. It is simply what separates functioning citizens from people who are not the best socialites. There has been much research on Emotional Intelligence and its applications and we will discuss this further in Chapter 2.

Chapter 2: What is Emotion and where does it come from?

An emotion is the instinctive state of mind resulting from external or internal stimuli. In the 20th Century, 6 basic emotions were decided upon by a psychologist named Paul Ekman. They are disgust, anger, sadness, joy, fear, and surprise. There are, of course, many emotions not mentioned in these six, but most of them will be experienced throughout your lifetime. It is said that our human emotions may be the result of evolution. Disgust for example, is what we teach our children to feel when they are around a dirty trash can or when they want to eat a piece of rotten food.

Speaking of evolutionary emotions, have you ever opened a drawer on a spider or stepped on a snake. The emotion of surprise is what tells our bodies to quickly get away from creatures that may bite us. It is fear that keeps us from placing ourselves in situations that will put us in danger. For each of these emotions, there is a dedicated circuit in our brains and it stems from a complex system of feelings and reactions.

These emotions are called "primary emotions". There are also, in contrast, complex emotions. Some of these complex emotions are humility, shame, nostalgia, and guilt. These emotions are mostly learned emotions, and they function more socially than for survival.

Complex emotions also have their own distinct circuits in the brain, and are more common in the later years of one's life.

Since these feeling have such a big effect on how we think and behave, scientists have spent a lot of time trying to figure them out. Our emotions are caused by thoughts. Often an external stimuli will internally cause us to think about the best reaction in response to how we feel about it. Even though multiple people may be in the same boat, they will more than likely differ in how they feel about it. This may be based upon previous learning and experience. For example, if you and your friend went to the lake to swim, your friend who has never swam in a lake before may be afraid that they will be bitten by a fish. You however, have swam in a lake before and you know that the fish in the lake will not bother you.

We know that obviously certain emotions are the result of certain types of thoughts, like when we think, " I feel like I am in danger," we feel fear in response. When we imagine something bad happening to us, we also feel afraid. Scientists have determined that these types of thoughts are what prepare us for our future. When we practice of response in our daily lives, we are becoming better prepared for situations that will arise in our later lives such as loss or anger. These types of questions have been found by scientists to answer questions like…

- Is what happened unexpected?
- Will I be able to cope with what happened?

- Is what happened going to make it easier or harder for me to get what I want?
- Is what happened enjoyable?
- Does what happened match with what I think is right and wrong?
- Is what happened my fault or someone else's?

Here is where we begin to look at our situations in a more positive light. It will make us feel sad when our ice cream machine breaks, but we will more than likely feel a lot sadder when we think we can do nothing to fix it. We can look at it in a more positive way however, and realize that there are probably many online resources that can show us how to fix our ice cream machine.

There is a phenomenon worth mentioning that I have not mentioned yet called " unconscious processing." Unconscious processing occurs when you feel an emotion, but you are not sure why. Our brains work a lot and do many things when we aren't paying attention. We do not notice the majority of what it is doing every day, and this includes triggering an emotion. It is a silly thought that your brain notices things that you can not consciously see happening, but it really does happen. If you catch yourself feeling a certain way and you aren't sure why you feel this way, try to think about what is happening around you… what is REALLY happening.

Unconscious emotions are a big part of why we have psychiatrists today to talk about how we feel. A psychiatrist is a person who is trained to listen to you and interpret your feelings in a way that perhaps you did not see before. It is wise to obtain an outside opinion on anything, and a psychiatrist can help you cope with things like loss, grieving a loved one, guilt, or trauma.

According to scientists, an "emotional reaction" has several parts.These parts do not necessarily happen in any order, but they happen when a new emotion is being experienced. Perhaps first, your brain will change how your body is functioning. When you are "struck with grief," often the common response is falling to your knees or needing to sit down. Grief is a powerful emotion and requires a lot of concentration. When one is grieving, the brain automatically prioritizes feeling that emotion and nothing else seems to matter. There are also positive reactions caused by the brain like smiling when you are happy and laughing when you are amused.

Another part of an emotional reaction is your brain causing you to think differently or focus on certain thoughts. When you are happy, your brain will focus on happy thoughts and things that bring you joy or make you smile, and when you are sad, you may feel the urge to listen to sad music or focus on sad thoughts. Think of the last time you remember feeling afraid. When you felt like you were in danger, do you remember your brain looking for other dangerous things? It's comparable to being on a roller coaster and being afraid that the tracks will break. You begin to flinch at every squeak you hear and very bump you feel. Your brain is consciously making you feel like you are in danger and you must be ultra aware of your surroundings.

A third part of your reaction may be the feelings and urges you get to act out or act differently than you normally do when you feel an intense emotion like fear or anger. You may shout or scream. This may be a part of depression as well. You could possibly feel like you want to stay locked inside of your house and avoid contact with the outside world.

Emotions come from your brain and they are a result of being a human being. Human beings are unique from all of nature because of the complex emotions we feel. They help us to socially interact with others and survive. There are many parts to an emotional reaction, and your emotions may be conscious or unconsciously felt, but overall we know that there are positive ways to deal with them.

Chapter 3: Studying Emotional Intelligence

Scientists have been studying emotional intelligence for quite some time. Humans are amazing because we are curious about ourselves, and I will further discuss some of the studies that have been conducted researching emotional intelligence and he applications of EQ in our daily lives.

In 2010, a study regarding general mental ability (GMA) and EQ was conducted using college students as models for academic and social performance. The study confirmed that EI and GMA had a direct effect on academic performance. It was determined, however, that GMA was a better predictor of how a student would perform from an academic standpoint than EI and GMA had a more direct relationship to grades and academic performance. The tradeoff to this finding was that EI alone was a predictor of social performance, and GMA was not found to correlate to social performance. EI was determined to single-handedly determine the quality of social interactions between college students and their peers.

We can gather from this study that mental ability does not cause one to be a better communicator or better friend. Even people with illnesses that cause low GMA are able to communicate well. Emotional intelligence is something that can be set aside when considering how well a student is doing in school, and so it is not nonsense when a parent claims that their child is intelligent even when they are showing poor grades. "Book smarts" are for sure a very different ball game than emotional intelligence, and it is certainly possible that a child may have a low GMA but high EQ.

In a separate study, individuals who had been diagnosed with Schizophrenia were given the Mayer-Salovey-Caruso Emotional Intelligence Test (MSCEIT). The subjects diagnosed with Schizophrenia scored poorly in comparison to the control group on the end total MSCEIT score. They also scored worse than the control group on 3 out of 4 subtests of the MSCEIT. There scores were worse when being evaluated on understanding, managing, and identifying emotions. Lower MSCEIT scores were directly in correlation to having a lower community functioning ability.

This study confirmed that individuals diagnosed with Schizophrenia have an impaired EI in comparison to a control group of individuals who do not have schizophrenia. They showed the most impairment in the understanding, managing, and identifying emotions sections. People with Schizophrenia in result have less social capabilities and a lower EI than the person who has not been diagnosed with Schizophrenia.

A third study by Nelis et. al (2009) was conducted to see if Emotional Intelligence can be taught, or in other words, they were researching whether it could possibly be a learned behavior. They divided the study participants into two groups and gave training to one of the groups for four sessions on EI. They gave the second group no training on EI.

After completion of the education, the group that received EI training showed significant increase in understanding and recognizing emotions when tested. This increase was considerably higher than the control group which did not receive training. They tested the groups again six months later, and found that the results were the same, and the group wit training had retained their abilities. The control group did not show a change after being tested a second time.

This study proved that Emotional Intelligence can be effectively taught, and has long-term effects on people who are receiving training. It is an example of how our school system can teach students to be more socially capable people in an effective manner. Emotional Intelligence training can also be applied in college and early education, and may even help people who have certain disorders that affect their ability to socially interact with others.

Research has proven that individuals who carry a high EQ are more likely to be successful. Emotional Intelligence is considered a crucial skill, and it directly involves your ability to communicate. The Center for Creative Leadership (CCL) has conducted research finding deficiencies in Emotional intelligence and emotional competence to be a primary cause of executive derailment.

The CCL determined that the three main reasons for failure are difficulty in handling change, inability to work well when separated into teams, and poor interpersonal relations. This conclusion was also confirmed via a study conducted by an International search firm called Egon Zehnder International. After studying 515 Senior Executives, they concluded that it was EQ that determined success and not IQ. They found that the senior executives who had high EQ had weak correlation with those who instead excelled in IQ, and they were more likely to succeed.

The CCL's study on EQ and individuals' likeliness to succeed can be compared to a study conducted by the Carnegie Institute of Technology (CIT) which researched EQ's correlation to financial success. The CIT credited 85% of financial successes with what they call "human engineering skills". These skills include personality traits, the ability to lead, the ability to negotiate, and the ability to communicate efficiently.

In addition to these findings, they also discovered that 15% of financial success was due to technical abilities. In conclusion, your social capabilities are more important than you technical skills, and being able to lead and communicate can vastly change your financial success. This proves emotional intelligence skills to be crucial skills.

Most of the studies performed on Emotional Intelligence have been performed within business type environments... more specifically, the executive leadership levels. When you are in a position of leadership, the value of Emotional Intelligence increases the higher you go. This is because the impacts of your actions or decisions are felt down the ladder of leadership and affects all levels of a business, though there have been studies which suggest that decisions on all levels are just as impactful and important.

These studies have all proven that people would much rather do business with people the like and trust. Emotional intelligence is a crucial skill, and among these skills are plenty of opportunities to be both successful in your career and successful in your financial life. Even though some illnesses (like schizophrenia) may impair your emotional intelligence skills and qualities, studies have confirmed that these skills can be efficiently taught. Perhaps this open the door to more opportunities to help people with these social illnesses to better themselves and learn to communicate better with others.

Chapter 4: Giving and Receiving Feedback

Feedback is essential to the growth of social and business type groups. It can be a positive way to improve as people or even as a family. It is essential though, that feedback is properly delivered in an uplifting and positive way. Negative feedback is never fun, but it is also important and it should always be constructive. Here are some stellar tips on giving and receiving positive and critical feedback.

Constructive criticism can be considered a good deed. You may use the sandwich effect to efficiently deliver suggestions in a positive and comfortable way. Place a negative observation between two good observations, and ask that they pay it forward. You should be comfortable creating an environment where constructive criticism is a natural, non-threatening form of communication between those who are in your daily environment. As long as your constructive criticism is being delivered thoughtfully, there will be nothing to feel threatened about. When you deliver constructive criticism at work, consider it a good deed and see it in a perspective that allows you to realize that you may have left them with a skill that will help them in their future lives and careers.

When giving feedback of any kind, you should always be specific and straightforward. It should be approached in a ay that is task-focused.

Try your best to refrain from comments that are general like, " You need to work better" or " Your work is not as good as it should be." Say things that are specific about their work such as, " When you turn in your documents, I have noticed that the formatting tends to be incorrect, and I believe you are using the wrong font each time." This critique was straight to the point and offered a solution without being rude. You have avoided confusing them or making them feel like you are picking on them. This method also gives them polite advice on how to improve themselves as an employee.

It is also important that you do not wait too long to give criticism. If you are in the mindset of, " I'll just wait until the next meeting/ family gathering," you need to throw that thought away! Criticism is immediately important and saves people embarrassment. Have you ever heard anything similar to, " Oh my goodness, why didn't anyone tell me my fly has been unzipped this entire time?" Waiting until a moment that you will feel more comfortable t deliver a bit of advice is unfair to the person you know is in need of constructive criticism. Criticize your colleagues or friends as mishaps occur. This will make them more comfortable to speak to you about their concerns and it will create an environment that makes people comfortable enough to ask questions.

Criticize them in private. Public critique is totally inappropriate always. The act of public embarrassment is cruel and uncalled for, so take them to another room if necessary, but do not ever feel the need to tell someone that they are doing something that is potentially embarrassing in front of others. Even when praising someone for good work, you should keep the meeting private. Some people do not like to feel like they are the focus of attention. Praise should be delivered in a straightforward fashion that is encouraging to them rather than annoying them with a public announcement. Perhaps a good way to deliver is by inviting them for a walk, or asking them to come to your office for good news.

Always end your feedback positively. This goes back to the sandwich method. Insert your criticism in between two compliments and be positive and constructive. Or instead, mention what needs to be worked on at the beginning of your conversation so that you may end with what you feel is a good thing about their work. If you end on a negative note, it erases any positive praise you gave them previous to the last comment. You should make them feel appreciated after you have stopped talking.

Have you heard of the 3x3 rule? This rule asks that each of your peers give 3 positive praise and 3 critiques for each other. This method was first introduced by Bert Decker in a book he authored called "You've Got to be Believed to be Heard." By focusing on 3 critiques at a time, you are setting a healthy pace for self-improvement while pairing them with 3 confidence boosters that will help to provide the motivation needed to begin improving.

It is is important also to keep your feedback strictly business and to make sure that you are critiquing work and not personality. If you dislike someone, that is okay, but don't let yourself sink to a level of allowing yourself to be controlled by your emotions. People who practice emotional intelligence are able to control and recognize their emotions. This is the perfect example of a moment you must be carefully aware of your emotions in. Say things like, "When your shirt is wrinkled and your collar is unbuttoned, you present an unprofessional appearance to the rest of the family." Do not say things like," Your laziness and ugliness is causing a problem." Focus on phrases which emphasize behavior and not personality.

Focus your feedback on efforts made individually rather than a broad statement which attempts to cover everyone. People want to be recognized for their efforts, and those who did a lot of the hard work know who they are. We as people crave recognition for our victories and efforts, so take the extra time to reach out individually, because if you can not properly measure individual efforts, you can not properly measure them.

Last but not least, allow yourself to be criticized. Take critiques with dignity and respect, and receive praise humbly. It makes the people around you more comfortable to speak with you when you give them opportunities to follow up on constructive criticism with your own performance and whether or not you can improve as a friend, boss, parent, or family member. You will find that receiving criticism is not so bad, and it builds character. There is nothing to be afraid of except fear itself, so be comfortable sharing your thoughts and feelings within a positive work environment. Do not give criticism in public, keep it truthful and straight to the point, and only include how someone can improve their behavior rather than insulting their personality.

Chapter 5: When you Need to Meet a Tight Deadline

Emotional intelligence allows one to effectively prioritize and manage time wisely. When we need to meet a deadline, it can sometimes be considered a huge factor considering the things that are causing us to feel stressed. It is not uncommon for stress alone to cause people to miss deadlines they could have easily met if there was not the level of anxiety present at the time they needed to be working. Lucky for us, there are a few tried and true ways we can manage our work to meet the deadlines we need and minimize stress while doing so.

First, you will benefit from caring about your deadlines instead of brushing them off to be non-important. Deadlines are crucial for work productivity and self-improvement. In other words, they get things done! It is lazy to wait until the last minute to begin working on a due project, and this is a terrible strategy! Recognize your deadlines as a firm goal, and give them the respect they are due. After all, meeting deadlines shows your employer that you are hardworking, and most importantly, a reliable asset to the team. Most employers hate tardiness more than anything else, and failure to meet a deadline could result in job termination or a bad work record.

Second, you should organize a list and keep it somewhere it will be seen everyday. Include in this list which projects you need to work on or finish and keep your list updated and accurate every day. Mark a calendar if you must and keep it on your desk. You can easily type up a to-do list on your computer or phone, or maybe consider placing sticky notes on your fridge. The point is, you should put in writing your projects and their due dates and make sure to look at and update it daily.

Thirdly, make sure that your deadlines are clear and accurate. Perhaps you weren't sure whether your boss will be angry if a project is a few days late, but maybe you did hear them correctly when they asked you to take your time. You want to be certain that your deadline will be reached in a timely manner and that you and your employer are on the same page. If the deadline is strict, shoot for a day before if possible, and if it is lax, also shoot for a day early, but feel free to continue improving the day it is due to be finished.

Fourth, prepare to finish your project a little earlier so that you may provide a cushion for your deadline. It may help to break down a project into several pieces and estimate how long each piece will take. If you think it is going to take a long time, make sure that your are still absolutely doing your best to finish at least a day to a few days before the deadline in order to ensure that you will not be finishing late. Also plan for delays. If you gave yourself a 3 day cushion and then came down sick with the flu, you could potentially take 2 days off and still have a day between your finished project and your deadline.

Fifth, be very clear on what is desired from you as a finished product. It would absolutely suck to work hard to finish something and then realize after it was too late that you created something that was not envisioned by your client or employer. Have a clear outcome and communicate with your boss! Most importantly, do not be afraid to ask questions about what it is that you are expected to be doing, and ask questions regarding your deadlines in relation to being ready to turn in your finished product. You may need a little extra time to deliver your finished product, or you may need to take into account how long it takes you to walk to the library and use their fax machine to turn in your work.

Turn your large project into smaller projects with a large outcome. Break your work down into smaller and simpler parts, and watch the time fly. Breaking down a project can help you get started when you do not know where to begin, and it can turn an intimidating piece of work into a less intimidating project that you can complete confidently and in a timely manner. Baby steps are a perfectly reasonable approach to a large project involving a tight deadline, and it will ensure that every piece of your finished project will have been focused on and finished with care.

Now that you have broken your large project into small pieces, focus on the first thing you will do to get started on your project. The first step you take will determine what your basis is to build other small tasks upon, and it will set the pace for your work. The fist step you take will feel satisfying after taking it, and it will motivate you to keep taking more steps. This way, you will be able to actively see your progress as you gp. This is a great method of staying motivated so go ahead and give that first little baby step your full attention and effort.

Next, you should be dedicating time in your work day to focus on the tasks that hold deadlines. Block your schedule to allow the adequate time needed to complete each important task and keep that time dedicated to its purpose devoid of distractions. Treat these time blocks like they are appointments, and start your work on time each day.

Now, say you know already that you will be missing your deadline. What do do you do, now? How do you professionally handle it? Of course the first option would be staying up very late trying to finish your project. If you know you were the cause, say perhaps by procrastination, you may just need to grab an energy drink or coffee and get it done. On the other side, you may have better luck negotiating a different deadline. It may have difficult to meet the first deadline because you overcommitted, which is a reasonable mistake. You should always be able to honestly and openly admit your mistakes. Whatever you do, be sure to meet your new deadline, because it is your responsibility to know what you can handle and overcommitting twice would be a bad mistake.

Chapter 6: What to Do When You Find Yourself in Need of Adaptation

Emotionally intelligent people have a knack for being adaptable. In a business environment, adaptability is a valuable trait. Resisting change brings us nowhere but right back where we started. You simply cannot resist it. In this chapter, we will discuss the importance of adaptation and how you can positively embrace the changes in your life.

Adaptation is an important skill because it allows you to make critical changes to your situation in order to adjust yourself to embrace new things. To adapt is to survive. Many years ago, our ancestors had to adapt to the harsh weather environment and build shelters and fires. Today, adapting might mean learning how to use a new piece of equipment for your job in order to keep up with the way factories are being ran. Adaptation can be marrying a man who has children and learning how to be a mother to a 5 year old. College students today have adapted by bringing smart devices, recorders, cameras, laptops, and other technological devices to class to help them do things like take notes or copy instructions and homework deadlines.

Change might be brought about by a crisis or a choice or maybe you just got lucky. You have a choice to make and you can decide to stay the same and not make any personal changes, or you can adapt. You can prepare yourself for change so that if and when it comes, you will be better prepared for it. These things allow you to take control of your life, and our lives most often find themselves reacting to change rather than creating it.

One method of adaptation is simply changing your mindset. Sometimes the reason we resist change is we feel more comfortable staying in situations that are familiar to us. Our subconscious mind dislikes the unknown future, so we aren't always fighting it on purpose. Change can be frightening, and it comes into our lives very suddenly. It disrupts our lives in harsh ways sometimes. Though we will not be able to control the pace or extremities of the change, we will always be able to control our reaction to it. Here we can practice seeing situations in more positive light. We will always be able to see something positive from every situation

Emotionally intelligent people try to find meaning in life. They step out of their comfort zones and realize that their comfort zones are the enemies of their achievements. You can find purpose in your life by taking the time to think about what you value. What things are important in your life? In order to properly be able to focus on how you plan to change for the better, you need the clarity of knowing your priorities and setting them straight. This way you will be able to manage your life and become more comfortable with change.

Research from the University of Missouri suggests that finding the meaning in life is less about meditation and years of harsh discipline, and more about self-awareness. Realizing that we are not on Earth for a very long time opens a door to new opportunities to truly feel alive. Live your life as if today might be your last. It does not require you to think super long or super hard about what life means. It only requires you to open your eyes to the answer that is already right in front of you. Once you find meaning in your life, adaptation will feel natural to you and you will no longer be a prisoner to your comfort zone.

Another consideration may be that successfully adapting to change requires us to let go of our past and our regrets and decide to actively live in the moment. Letting go of your regrets is key to being able to face change in a brave and willing fashion. You will find that your past regrets have an impact on your ability to step out of the cocoon you have built around you for comfort, and in order to move on you need to first let go.

If you continue to focus on your past, you will miss new opportunities to grow and become a better, more emotionally intelligent person. You simply won't be able to recognize a memory from an open door. Opportunities after all, are presented by the events of change. Remember and remind yourself that you can not change the past, but you will alway be able to change your future for the better. Maybe try writing a letter to your past self and writing down all of the regrets that you may have. Then, if you feel it is necessary, burn the letter or rip it into tiny pieces.

Lastly, a great method of adapting is simply being ready for it. Prepare yourself for the changes happening in your life. Think of all the things that scare you, and then go do them. Cross them off of your list. You may find that you are a lot braver than you think you are, and practicing bravery is nothing to be ashamed of. Showing yourself that you have the motivation to take active steps toward a better life will allow you to keep improving your life for the rest of your time on Earth.

Focus on living a life that is healthy. Always remember to do you. If you need to take a break from change, take a break. It is far better to be well rested so that you can more efficiently finish a task than to be upset and tired and lose motivation

Adaptation is less scary than it looks, yet easier said than done. Just know that by making positive changes in your life, you are setting yourself up for more opportunities and a better time being alive. This is something that people who are emotionally intelligent do., and you can always try again if at first you do not succeed.

Chapter 7: How to cope with Change

Now that we have talked about adaptation and why it is important to have the skills necessary, let's further discuss how to deal with change. Change is sometimes not a positive thing, like losing a loved one, and it can be very difficult and take a long long time to overcome a forced change in your life like this. Emotionally intelligent people still have a difficult time coping with change sometimes, and we will discuss positive ways you can cope with change and move on.

What is the worst that could happen? Sometimes we have a difficult time coping with change because we are overthinking the consequences. We can be afraid of the unknown, or afraid to leave our past behind. The past can be comfortable, and it is sometimes hard to imagine ourselves living in an environment that is no longer similar to our past. Have you ever faced a challenge like this one and made it through alright? Think about maybe the first time you drove a car alone, or the first day of your first job. This is more than likely not the first time your have dealt with change and the worst that could happen is probably only existent as an extreme, scary thought in your mind. If you are a visual learner, you could possibly benefit from writing down what you are afraid of and then rationally considering the probability of these things happening. It may take some time to become comfortable, but you will eventually get used to this new way of living.

Be certain also of how much you can handle on your own. If you can not handle this change on your own, the intelligent thing to do would be asking for help. You can take this opportunity to recognize your emotions and realize that they are too extreme for you to deal with alone. There is no shame in asking for help. Also, you should be aware of how much of this change you can actually control. You can not control the event which led to the calling for change, but you can control your reaction and you can control which direction you choose to be moved by this event. Put these things in perspective by making a mental to-do list and checking off each item as it is completed.

Next, accept the change and embrace it in a positive perspective. Imagine your kitchen catching fire. Your kitchen catching fire is obviously never a great thing, but hey, art least now you get to buy a new stove like you have been putting off. You already know that you can only control so much, and what is done is done. So embrace this opportunity to better the situation in a creative, satisfying way. Even when it is difficult to cope, embrace this opportunity to learn and grow. It will benefit you in the end to do your best to avoid seeking the negatives from the situation and dwelling on them.

After you have accepted the change in your life, focus on and celebrate the positives in it, too. You will be able to manage the change when you take a break from the unfortunate things happening to you and prioritize the good things you still have. Think about your friends and you famil… your loved ones. The positive things in your life might not be obvious at first, but if you begin to look for them, you will find them. Try to make the best of this situation, and remember that you have friends and loved ones who are ready to support you.

Another way to cope with change is to take action and take control of your life, Again, the path you are following is something you CAN control, so grasp it firmly and take it by the horns. Begin to clean up the mess and get up and call your loved ones when you are feeling sad or having difficulties. You are not alone in this and you are not helpless. Even when success does not immediately come, you will always have tomorrow, and the next day, and the next. Don't forget that Rome wasn't built in a day, and the sun is not going to stop coming up no matter what, so like the sun, keep moving forward.

Most importantly, when coping with a difficult change, manage your stress. Emotionally intelligent people are good at managing their emotions and knowing when too much is too much. It does not make you a better or a tougher person to keep going when you know that you should take a break instead. Try making a cup of tea, or simply take a break. Maybe a vacation is what you need after a catastrophic event, but what you do not need is frustrating yourself into giving up. You must keep moving forward at all costs, but this doesn't mean you can not work at your own pace. Try being more mindful of your actions, and practice self-awareness.

Lastly, I will emphasize a second time, seek support from your supporters. You do not have to do this alone, and it shows good character to be able to admit when you can not handle change by yourself. Share your journey with others so that when they are facing similar challenges, they will be able to find comfort knowing that they are not alone, and they are not the first one to go through something like this. Let others know also when you are okay. Reassure them that this change is not going to halt your entire life, but also be honest and open about what it is you may be struggling with and you feel about it.

Coping with change can be difficult, but through seeking help and support, focusing on the positives, and prioritizing what is important to you, you can positively take the actions necessary to get through this. You are most likely not the first one and others have gone through something similar. Just let yourself relax and take a minute to breathe when needed and know that you are not alone and you can do this!

Chapter 8: Managing and Coping with your failures and Setbacks

Let's be honest. Nobody enjoys failing, but failure is one of the most crucial steps to becoming successful. We learn more things from failing than anything else. It is one of the most powerful learning tools in existence, and even though it might set you back, emotionally intelligent people are able to cope with failure in ways that healthy. These ways of overcoming failure involve several traits of a person with a high EQ such as mindfulness, self-awareness, the ability to manage your emotions, and logically thinking before acting. These methods of dealing with setbacks below should shine some light on what I mean.

First, recognize your emotions and accept how this makes you feel. Recognize that you may be angry and upset, but also make sure that you think hard about how you are going to react. It is okay to have these feelings. You have a right to feel the way you feel. Just know that these feelings do not control you and you always have the ability to choose how you are going to react. Do not swallow your feelings, they will still be there when you come back from pretending that they aren't. These impulses can be strong, because you may feel ashamed or be embarrassed, but it is not the best option for you to do something like that.

Allow yourself to hurt and allow yourself to heal.

Do not label yourself as a failure just because you had a minor setback. One failure is not going to continue to lead to many more, and it is not going to affect you for the rest of your life if you refuse to allow it. YOU are not the product of your failure, but your failure is a product of you. It is a product of you giving a genuine effort to become better or create something new. This sort of look on life is destructive, and affects you only when you allow it to affect you. If you think about it in a more positive light, you may find that the things you learned today may lead you to success next time. See your failure as temporary, and remember that failure is the sign of someone who genuinely tries.

This brings us to the next part, learning from your failures. A failure is a learning opportunity, and it should be treated as such. What is at least one or two things you can think of that you learned from this. Did you learn to study harder, or perhaps use a different plan of action? Did you make an embarrassing mistake, that you know to never make again? You may have to think for a little while, but you will definitely find that you learned something. Think about how you will avoid making this mistake a second time. You will best benefit from being constructive with your answers and realizing that you can avoid these mistakes next time. Most importantly, make sure that you try again.

Remember and remind yourself that failure is only a very natural part of becoming anyone in life. Anyone who wants to become anyone has to first pass through a trial of errors. I know that you get discouraged by hearing of others successes while you feel like a failure, but they did not hop into the winner car and ride away into the sunset without first scraping a few knees and elbows. You are going to be okay. One day, you can be successful, too, but you have to pick yourself up, dust yourself off and try again. "Success is the result of perfection, hard work, learning from failure, loyalty, and persistence." - Colin Powell

It is also worth mentioning that bottling up your feelings and not allowing yourself to grieve naturally is going to do much more harm than good for you. Let it out. Tell other people who you trust about your feelings. This is nothing to be ashamed of. You may be embarrassed, but you will not be remembered by this. If you choose to tell someone, venting is a great way to feel and then expose your emotions. You deserve to tell someone how you feel and you deserve to feel the way you do. It can be very helpful to have someone who cares listen to you talk about your feelings.

Find inspiration in your surroundings to move on from this setback and try a different route. The people who are supporting you may have some stellar recommendations, so listen to the people you trust. A conversation with someone you trust can be the difference that inspires you to try again in a different way. Try to find strength in the enthusiasm and optimism of the people rooting you on. They believe in you and they know you can do it if you try hard enough. These people don't even have to be close to you or anyone you know personally. Try reading a book or online article on failure. Read other people's stories regarding their setbacks and their success stories, or maybe even watch a video online.

After you find the inspiration to get up again, keep moving forward. Do not wear handcuffs tied to this setback. You have accepted this situation for what it is, and you have told yourself that you are not a failure yourself. Now it is the time to move forward and leave your failure in the past. It may feel like swimming in mud, but you've got this! Make a plan and execute it. Do you know how to move on from here? Maybe you do not even need to start again from the very beginning. At least this time you might have a foot already facing the right direction! Look at the positives and start working!

Alright so you have created a plan on moving forward, how will you execute it. You are at the stage of a setback that is in the moving on part, so get to work. Are you going to bring more people into the project or are you going to try again by yourself? Have you listened to the advice you were given? Your plan for moving forward doesn't need to be perfect, but it needs to be well-thought out. If your plan seems like a handful, split it into simpler parts and celebrate each part you finish. Again, this plan does not need to be outstandingly perfect. The important thing here is that you are trying again and this time, you have a plan.

Lastly, believe in yourself and tell yourself that you can overcome this failure. You have communicated your feelings and you have felt your emotions. Now this is the time you can really show yourself and others what you are made of. You are fire, baby! This failure WILL NOT drag you down or make you feel like you no longer wish to try. You are as good as you believe you are when your belief is paired with an equal amount of determination.

Chapter 9: Keeping the Intelligent Body Healthy

Emotional intelligence comes with things like a healthy lifestyle and a healthy brain. Now, I am not referencing a healthy body that is healthy because it runs 3 miles every day and drinks protein shakes. I am talking about your Emotional body. Our mind is as complex as a thousand spider webs tangled together in an intricate pattern only a spider knows. It requires care and stimulation. It is eager to feel extreme emotions and it is excited to learn new things each day. Human beings are perhaps the most interesting creatures because of our emotional bodies, and it is interesting that we are the only animals who truly understand our own minds and the capabilities of its functioning, yet we have really only began to scratch the surface. Let's discuss how you can keep your emotionally intelligent body happy and healthy.

Our emotional bodies crave stimulation. There is a lot of energy to be burned in a healthy body. Scientists have found the mental stimulation causes your brain to make new connections and it even helps it to build new cells. These new cells help the plasticity of your brain. Your brain is almost unlimited on the amount of information you can plug into it. Things like reading and writing, watching educational films, doing puzzles, and going out all help your brain to grow and increase its functional ability. The more stimulation you feed your brain, the more new cells it creates, and this can make a considerable difference when you are older and your brain is beginning to lose cells.

Now your body needs physical exercise. A healthy heart that can pump blood to your brain is a valuable asset to the team. Scientists have found that muscle usage over time not only keeps your body young, but your mind as well. Getting your blood pumping helps oxidate your body and leave your muscles ready to go to work the next day. Not to mention, physical exercise keeps your weight stable, and it makes you feel good. Exercise will also do things like lower your blood pressure, enhance your mood, improve the levels of cholesterol in your body, and help your blood sugar stay at a healthy level.

Eat brain healthy foods! A healthy diet keeps your body happy and makes you feel more energetic throughout the day. Some of us are guilty of surviving off of coffee and donuts, but next time try a balanced breakfast including fruits. If you drink coffee, that's fine, but maybe try black coffee with a little cream. Try to avoid the tempting sugar-filled Cappuccinos and Macchiatos. Go for the healthier option. Coffee itself is not bad for you, it helps to wake your body up and can be an alternative to energy drinks or laxatives. It aids with metabolism and can help you use the restroom. Just try to be careful avoiding the sugar syrups and creams that we sometimes put into our coffee.

A healthy mind requires a healthy blood pressure. Blood pressure is important because it helps your blood to reach the extreme parts of your body like your toes and fingers. Extremely low blood pressure can make you pass out, and high blood pressure can overwhelm the body making you feel weak and dizzy. Blood pressure is a delicate balance, and what you are eating and how much exercise you are getting matters. High blood pressure when you are young greatly increase the chance that you will have a larger decline in mental health as you age. Keep your blood pressure low and healthy to save your brain!

Now let's talk about blood sugar. Like blood pressure, blood sugar levels will also tend to make you feel weak and dizzy or even pass out if they are not carefully balanced. Be aware of how much sugar you are eating everyday and watch your sodium intakes. You may be surprised at what foods can actually carry a lot of sugar like ketchup and again, different arrangements of coffee. Diabetes greatly affects the mind and it cause you to become slow thinking and even forgetful. Consider the fact that diabetic people are at a greater risk of dementia. Also, if your blood sugar reaches levels that are too high, you may develop the type of diabetes that requires medication to keep it at healthier levels, and it can be a very difficult thing to overcome.

Cholesterol also affects the brain. Bad cholesterol is called" LDL". High levels of this type of cholesterol are another thing that has been previously associated with an increased risk of dementia. The things you can do to keep your cholesterol levels healthy are the obvious things like diet and exercise. Keeping your weight down also affect your cholesterol… in a positive way. Sometimes weight management is a difficult thing. Some of us just simply do not have the type of metabolism that others have, but you can ask your doctor for help.

Maybe you should consider the things you can do everyday that are small, but make a difference, like taking vitamins. Taking vitamins can ensure that your body is getting what it needs if your diet is lacking in that department. Things like vitamin C and folic acid help to keep your mind healthy and they increase the likelihood that your body will fight off things like the flu bug. Consider taking a daily aspirin. Aspirin helps to keep your blood pressure at a healthy level and it can lead to an increase in vascular health. There have also been studies which suggest low-dose aspirin decreasing the likelihood of developing dementia in later life.

A very important thing you can do for your brain also is avoiding things you know are bad for you, like tobacco, marijuana, and excessive amounts of alcohol. Excessive drinking severely limits the amount of oxygen that is reaching your brain. Being drunk is a form of histotoxic hypoxia. This means that you are limiting the supply of oxygen to your brain, and you are reaching a point that there is not enough oxygen to function properly. This can be dangerous and even lead to heart failure. Alcohol is addictive, so you need to stop when you know you have had enough. Tobacco leaves a lot of nasty things in your lungs that are in turn carried on your blood cells to the brain as well. You don't want that nasty tar in there, trust me.

Do you know that marijuana usage has several negative long term impacts on your brain? The truth is, most people begin smoking and ingesting marijuana when they are young enough to still have 4 or 5 years of brain development left. Weed smoking can stunt the growth of your brain and frequently causes teens to fail out of school. The use of weed causes your brain to refuse to have a normal functioning of the parts that affect memory and learning. A study conducted in rats showed that when given THC, the rats soon found that they enjoyed the feeling, and after an extended amount of time, they no longer felt the level of high that they wanted, so they began to self-administer more dangerous drugs when given the chance.

Doing anything to purposefully impair yourself mentally is extremely damaging to your EQ, and it is never a wise thing to do for entertainment. It reduces the connectivity in your brain and causes you to lose precious cells that you will never gain back. Weed and alcohol and tobacco all greatly increase the likelihood of cardiac disease and even cardiac failure. Just don't do it.

Lastly, take care of your emotional health. If you are feeling alone or depressed, it is best to reach out for help, even when you feel like you may bother others or cause someone to no longer enjoy being around you. These irrational thoughts are never a reason to continue letting yourself feel like you alone. Do your best to be happy, and know that it is okay if you aren't. Happy times will come again as long as you keep looking forward and let the past be the past. These things will help you better take care of your emotionally intelligent body.

Chapter 10: Becoming Self-aware

Developing self awareness may take time, but it is so worth it. You will begin to see the areas of yourself that need work and you will find that working on them is not such a bad thing. Being self-aware means that you have a grasp on who you are and how you are feeling. You be able to take a good guess on how the things you say and do will affect others around you. It is a good idea to think about how you are really feeling because then you can hold yourself accountable.

Self awareness is the basis of a person who has strong character and integrity. It creates leaders, people you can trust. These people are always honest with themselves, and you can be honest with them, too. Leaders who are self-aware are able to seek and find any gaps in their abilities and fix the problem quickly and efficiently. Self awareness opens your mind to the possibility of needing work, and it solves problems in a quick and easy way. As a leader, becoming aware of yourself and your emotions can more effectively help you make decisions concerning others. It saves a lot of regret when you can recognize that you are angry, and cool down before completely melting your throat to someone out of anger.

Self awareness in the education setting has a positive impact on both student and educators. Being a self-aware student helps you focus on what you may be lacking and what you need to study more of. It's like thinking about your thinking. You should be able to reflect on and evaluate yourself as a student without upsetting yourself over trivial things that may just take a few minutes to understand. Calmly acknowledge what you find difficult and brainstorm on how you might better understand it. This way you are not only bettering yourself as a student in the aspect of academic performance, but you are also bettering yourself as a learner.

So how do you increase your self awareness? First, you should view yourself objectively. Try to view the raw, uncensored version of you… your true self. Sometimes this isn't easy when we have self-esteem issues, but you can learn to love yourself for who you are. Maybe take some time to reflect on the things that you like so that maybe you can really get to know yourself. Getting to know yourself can be rewarding, and it can help you quit bad habits. For example, if you know you shouldn't be eating a ton of sweets right now for your health, but you often feel pressured to order dessert when going out with your friends because they order dessert, knowing yourself and realizing that your friends won't think you are less fun because you made a decision for your health can be liberating.

Perhaps try to listen to what your friends think of you, and let them know they can be honest. Reflect on things you have done that made you feel good about yourself, such as finishing an art project, writing a book, or losing weight. It will help to understand what sort of things bring you true joy and what things bring you false joy. True joy may be seeing your friends or your family. False joy might be binge-watching a TV show in your room because you are bored. You should be giving more effort to find something that you truly want to be doing.

Self awareness can be discovered also by keeping a journal. Writing is a huge stress reliever for many people, and you can always tell a journal whatever you want to tell it. A journal will never share your secrets, so you may find that you are writing about things you previously felt uncomfortable discussing with your friends or trusted family members. Doing this can really bring out some feelings or thoughts that you did not consciously know you had before. You may realize that you had lied to yourself about some things, and now you have opened your mind to the possibility of addressing these things and bettering yourself.

In this journal you might write down some things like your goals, your desires, and your dreams. Sometimes we forget who we are, and it takes a little reminiscing to really remember why we started this journey in the first place. These ideas and these desires can help you realize that you are a better person than you tell yourself you are. You have so many beautiful aspirations and visions for who you want to be, so you should go out and reach for these goals. There is nothing stopping you but yourself, and that is something you must realize on your own.

Realizing how to become self-aware is going to take some daily reflection. What was today like? How did work go? Did I handle the situations today in a professional or appropriate manner? Remember the things you did today that were good and bad. Is there more good than bad? Why were some things bad? Self-reflection can include time you take writing in your journal. (Notice how the journal keeps being mentioned here. It is more important than you will know until you keep one.) Today's world demands that we take in a little and pump out a lot, so take the time every day to focus on yourself and reflect on how you felt that day.

There are a few habitual things that involve relaxing that you can do to practice mindfulness, like meditation or simply laying down and thinking of how you feel. Relax your body, close your eyes, and focus on your breathing. Ask yourself how you feel. Self-awareness comes from within. It is something you have to realize for yourself; no one knows you like you do. By becoming self-aware, you will know yourself better and learn to know others better. It is all a part of the journey that you have to take to find out who you are on the inside. Once you familiarize yourself with yourself, you become your true self.

Chapter 11: Neuroscience and its Connection to your Emotions

The term "emotion" is described differently by a lot of people. Sometimes if you ask someone what they think an emotion is, they picture in their mind the physical actions that often accompany emotions. Others may think of their own feelings and remember how they felt the last time they had a strong emotion. Some scientists believe that emotions can be studied only in humans because they are so complex. In contrast, others can find that animals and even insects are capable of exhibiting the behaviors of an emotional being. The emotional state can be broken down and studied in groups of neuroscientific topics, and here we will discuss the ways your emotions are tied with the physical traits of your brain.

There are a handful of scientists who agree that different emotions come from very specific anatomical parts of the brain. They believe that the different sections of your brain are responsible for triggering very specific emotions, and each emotion is only capable of being triggered by that part. Though, some scientists will insist that your emotions are triggered by random parts of your brain, and there is no correspondence between which emotion is triggered and which part of the brain has fired. In the midst of these vastly contrasting arguments, there is a third group of scientists who passively believe that your emotions are simply a consequence of your behavior, and not a cause of it.

Ralph Adolphs and David J. Anderson, authors of the book, The Neuroscience of Emotion, both say that they believe you can only begin to create a testable hypothesis and form a reasonable opinion on emotions after you can clearly define what an emotion is. Adolphs studies human social behavior, more specifically focusing on the neural basis. Anderson uses rodents and fruit flies to experiment how internal organisms' internal states trigger their own emotional behaviors. Their published journal is a conceptual outline for studying emotional behaviors in humans and other animals.

As described in their book, " emotions are biological phenomena that cause behavioral and physiological changes in the brain and body and—in some species—subjective feelings." They go on further to say that as long as emotions are classified in ways that are measurable, the neurobiological implementation of these states can be studied. They may be investigated separately from subjective conscious feelings, so both animals and humans may be candidates for investigation.

The brain is the most demanding organ you have in your body, since it requires the most blood and the most oxygen. There are thousands of complicated neural networks inside of your brain that help you function everyday. The brain can also be divided into sections that each serve a purpose like storing memories.

There are three areas of the brain that are used to describe its functions. There is lizard brain, mammal brain, and human brain. The lizard brain is the deep part of your brain that focuses on survival. Its priority is keeping you alive. Most of the functions in the lizard brain are unconscious. They involve breathing, beating your heart, and digesting food. It is referred to as, "lizard brain" because it represents the most primitive part of our functioning brain. This is the instinctual part of your brain that is primarily used when you are an infant to help you feel things that help you survive like fear and disgust.

Did you ever touch a stove as a child? Or were you afraid of the dark? Do you remember yanking your hand away quickly and maybe putting your finger in your mouth? Or did you jump and scream when you heard something fall over that you couldn't see? All of things result from your lizard brain. These are your survival instincts. Steven Pressfield calls the lizard brain a tool of "resistance". He believes that the lizard brain disables us from being the best version of ourselves. In his book, he describes it as something that is primitive and has hardly evolved. He says it, "does more harm than good.".

Outside of the lizard brain, we have what is called the limbic system, or "mammal brain". Your limbic system concerns itself with you safety by storing memories of the past that involved pleasure and pain. The mammal brain also urges you to repeat things that involve pleasure, kind of like when you only want to eat *one more* piece of candy, but you finish the entire bag instead. We call this part of the brain the "mammal brain" because it is unique to mammals. It helps you feel pleasurable emotions and learn from your mistakes.

Now the human brain is the most recently evolved piece of your cortex. It is called the "neocortex". It is located at the front of your brain and houses our conscience. This is where our thinking occurs. The human brain is very responsible for learning, decision making, thinking, and rationalizing. This part also controls your nervous system. It receives information from your nerves and send it back to your muscles. It is responsible for telling you if something is really hot or sharp.

You brains networks get stronger or weaker depending on how often they are used. This way you can overcome fear and anxiety and live your best life. When we feel emotions, they can sometimes make us afraid, like, "why am I feeling this way?" Your brain parts do not agree 100% of the time. Sometimes you might really want to do something, or try something new. Your human brain might tell you that skydiving looks like a lot of fun, but your mammal brain disagrees and tells you that it is unsafe.

The brain can both give us an emotion in response to a stimuli, or cause a behavior by giving us an emotion first. Your brain may give you a memory of something that makes you really angry and causes you to do something irrational like punching a wall. Your brain may even put you into a mood, where an emotion stays and lingers for a while.

There is an interesting theory that a feeling and an emotion are two different things. This theory states that emotions are different than feelings in that your brain can rationalize your feelings, but not your emotions. An emotion, in this case, is more primitive and happens quickly. It is an easy and quick reaction. Your feelings however, are the combination of your thoughts and your emotions. It is something that develops over a period of time and eventually leads to a mood.

In conclusion to this chapter, neuroscience is very closely related to our feelings and emotions. Emotions are, in fact, partially physical in that they are caused by your brain. Your brain is what reminds you what makes you feel bad or feel good. You can control, it but it takes practice and time. After all, we are only human.

Chapter 12: Behaving in the Workplace

Most of us are excited to be hired at a new job. We have ambition, and we want to see ourselves rising through the executive ladder. Or sometimes we might be getting a job after it has been a while, and we aren't sure how to behave at work. The ways you behave at work will determine whether your coworkers like you, and can help you get the things you want, like promotions. Here are some ways you can rock your work uniform and get people to enjoy working with you.

First, you should practice good character. Good character means that you make an effort to be a decent person. You do not lie, steal, or cheat, and you are always polite. Someone who has good character has a lot of integrity as well, and they radiate a sense of trust. You should try your best to be decent at the least, and carry yourself in a manner not too prideful, but definitely confident. Good character is something that makes you a likeable person. It gives you a reason to get up every morning with a smile on your face and a can-do attitude.

You should try to master a skill or a set of skills that sets you apart from your coworkers. Being the go-to person at work for something carries a lot of responsibility and opportunity to sort of brag on yourself. It feels good to be told you are good at something, and learning new skills and becoming good at them keeps you valuable to your work team. Do not be afraid to learn new skills to adapt to your job. Adaptation shows your boss that you are able to dedicate yourself to your job when your job calls for you to change.

When you feel your peers are not learning as easily or as quickly as you, share your knowledge with them. If they are expressing interest in " how you do it," kindly explain to them what they would like to learn and stay humble about it. Nobody likes to work with a know-it-all, but they do enjoy working with intelligent people who seem to know what they are talking about. If you can show your supervisor that you have not only mastered these skills, but you are now helping others to grow, you can exhibit to them that you are the perfect candidate for leadership positions within the company.

Be a dependable worker. Your boss and your coworkers are relying on you to show up on time and do quality work. Being late for work once is not the end of the world, but making a habit can be the end of your job. Not only is arriving on time an important trait, but being prepared for work is, too. You should never come to work unprepared when you knew you had the time and resources to be ready before-hand. This is never good. Show everyone that you have what you need and you are aware of what is going on.

Be a positive, radiant person. Showing up for work with a bad attitude leaves a sour taste in everyone's mouth. They might label you as a dislikable person, a label that is not easily peeled off. Try to help your coworkers feel better about their day and smile when you greet them.

Sometimes the solution to not enjoying being at work is to just choose positivity. Maybe one way you could choose positivity is wearing bright-colored, interesting clothes to work. There have been scientific studies finding that your mood is tied to the clothing you wear.

Also, take ownership and responsibility for your mistakes. Remember when we talked about having good character? This is where that applies. If you make a mistake, more than likely it wasn't too bad. You may find that everyone will be much more forgiving than you had anticipated. Don't allow yourself to convince your brain that you need to lie about what really happened to save yourself from the wrath of your boss. It may hurt to tell the truth, but it will hurt a lot less than being caught in a lie. So be yourself and be responsible.

Be proactive and start with the end result in your mind. You can fill the needs as you see them. Procrastination helps no one and causes mass panic, so do your best to start early and come to work prepared. It shows your boss and your coworkers that your character is not that great when you are constantly procrastinating. People who hire you want to see that you are a go-getter, not a lazy susan. Try your best to be ahead of the game.

Never send emails you couldn't show to your boss, and never make jokes you couldn't share with everyone. HR departments take jokes seriously when they involve discrimination or prejudice humor. Remember that everything you put on the internet stays there. If someone you didn't get along with got a hold of this email, it can very quickly be the end of your career, and even damage the reputation of your employer. Just don't do it. Do your best to keep your emails clean, and professionally formatted. In the end, it's better to tell these jokes outside of work or on a day off rather than risking everything you have for a quick laugh with your work friends.

Another thing you should refrain from doing is distracting others from their work. You will have chances to converse and socialize during your break, but do not cause your coworkers to mess up their job. Things like clown-like behavior and excessive talking can make your coworkers work worse or slower, and your boss can see that you are causing problems. Recognize that sometimes you have the urge to be the center of attention, and overcome these urges. Learn to be solemn and content with waiting for your break to be social. You can distract yourself with work or listening to music if it helps you resist the urge to start being too relaxed with your friends.

Here is an important rule to follow. Keep your work life and your personal life separate. No one at work wants to listen to you continue on and on about your toe infection. Conjoining your work life with your personal life can be something that causes you to lose your job because not only can it cause you to become annoying, but it can often lead to oversharing details that are not appropriate to bring u while at work. You can talk about some things with your work friends when you feel that they are comfortable discussing it and they are interested, but if you can tell that it makes them feel uneasy, you are best off getting a therapist instead!

While at work, never harass or bully any of your coworkers. Sometimes you might not be aware that you are harassing them, they may not always tell you that what you've said or done really hurt them, but if they were to tell the Human Resources dept. or your boss first, the consequences for you would not be pretty. Do your best to treat others at work how you expect to be treated. Avoid excessive name-calling, making too many jokes about one person, and never ever put your hands on another co-worker in a jokingly violent way. These things are very serious.

Also, do your best not to whine and complain about everything all the time. Whining is awful and employers really dislike it. You can not show up to work with a negative attitude and keep that attitude the entire time while doing quality work. A completely negative outlook on work encourages others to be negative and eventually, they will trace the negativity back to you. Complaining is also annoying, so just don't do it. Do not be the guy that everyone avoids because you only open your mouth when you're ready to say something hateful.

In the end, keep your profession professional. Be a positive and reliable person. Your boss will notice when you are doing a good job, so you don't have to let everyone know about it all the time. Be a good worker and respect other good workers.

Chapter 13: Culture and its Effects
on your Brain

Researchers from MIT have found that people from different cultures approach problem solving in different ways. There exists an interdisciplinary branch of neuroscience called, " cultural neuroscience." CN researches the different way the brain is affected due solely on which culture you come from. Culture is both constructed by and constructing our minds all over the world. It seems that our brain's' plasticity has something to do with it. Plasticity is your brain's ability to adapt to a long-term effect and evolve to survive it. These scripted behaviors become familiar to it, and it builds its neural networks to fit the appropriate situation.

We know from previous research that the hippocampi of our brains is the area that undergoes physical changes by repetition of everyday behaviors. Previous fMRI studies have uncovered exactly how your cultural background can influence the neural activity within your more complex areas during many different cognitive functions. Resulting from these studies, we know that cross-cultural differences in brain activity among Western and East Asian participants have been revealed during different daily, repetitive tasks including visual perception, attention, doing simple maths, and self-reflection. The brain changes occured due to the accumulated experiences the participants had from their own culture over time.

Your psyche is affected also by things we do that are pertinent to our time. For example, reading is an important tool for the developing mind and it is important that young children are encouraged to read. Reading does some pretty amazing things to our brain, like being prompted to create a picture or sounds in our minds by looking at words. This teaches children how to use their imagination, which is very important for the development of problem-solving skills as an adult. In some research, it was found that children could identify what was happening in a picture faster by simply reading its caption instead of looking at the picture directly.

Some research even suggests that studying a culture, and reading about it, is almost the same as living it. Our brains are so immensely powerful and amazing that they are able to store information from second sources just as well as it is stored from a direct source. The funny thing is, scientists have found that our brains do not distinguish differences between reading about an experience and actually living it. When you are reading, it has been scientifically deemed accurate that the same neurons in your brain are activated when you are experiencing something first hand. If you read about something a long time ago, you may recently have found that you had a difficult time remembering if you read it or actually saw it.

Moving between two cultures also has the potential to physically alter the brain. Your hippocampus and cerebral cortex are both know to grow in size when learning a new language. The brain grows larger with the amount of effort and dedication you put into learning. When you begin reading labels at the market in a different currency and learning how to count change with different coins than you first learned, these repetitive daily tasks fire the neurons in the hippocampus and the plasticity of your brain allows you to physically adapt to fit your new living environment.

According to *Forbes*, the most emotionally aware country is the Philippines. A study conducted in the 2000's found that only 60% of Filipinos, however, had felt they have felt the full range of possible human emotions. The countries that were the least emotionally aware only experienced about 30%. The United States only had 54% of the population claim that they had felt the full emotional range. When compared to others, it seems the United States is one of the least emotionally aware countries of the top 10, but still pretty emotionally aware. One of the least emotionally aware countries is, surprisingly, Singapore

Culture changes your personality. People from similar cultures share similar personality traits. Anthropologist Franz Boas created a theory called "Cultural Relativism" explaining the relationship between culture and one's personality. He argues that personality is less dependent on biology than people originally thought, and that it instead depends on the culture you were surrounded with when growing up. His student furthered his studies by expanding on Cultural patterns and themes. The research conducted by both found that more primitive tribes of people have closely held their cultural personalities together through many years by valuing their beliefs and rituals. These tribes teach their children to also value these things, and since they have little opportunity to be influenced by any outside sources, their personalities remain extremely similar to each other. In fact, they have had similar personalities to those people in their tribes who lived generations ago.

We know that culture affects the brain and your personality. Switching between two cultures can have a big impact on your emotional intelligence, and you may find yourself discovering pieces of your personality you didn't know you had in you. Experiencing different parts of the world is a great way to find who you really are through interacting with people different than you, and seeing sights you never thought you would see in person. The world and the anthropology it contains is beautiful, and it is recommended by psychologists that you try to experience it for yourself.

Chapter 14: Learning to Lead, and Why Emotionally Intelligent People make the Best Leaders

The self- awareness and problem solving skills found in people who are considered to be emotionally intelligent make them to be impeccable leaders. Emotionally intelligent people are often the ones who don't mind stepping up and volunteering to take charge. A leader is someone who takes charge and can be trusted to steer his or her followers in the right direction. Psychologists today can agree that we need more leaders in the world, which is why curriculum in schools promoting emotional intelligence is so important. Below we will discuss how one becomes a leader, and why these traits make a person more fit to lead.

Leaders are team players. Teamwork is vital to not only the quality of your work, but in more extreme cases, survival. Building a team takes advantage of everyone's collective talents and helps you finish projects in a timely manner, So when working in a team, a good team player knows their strengths and weaknesses. They have something to bring to the table. You are more than likely trying to build a team because it is going to take more than one person to tackle this issue, so do your best to use your strengths. Put yourself out there and let your teammates know that you are really outstanding at something, and most importantly, show up and give effort.

Secondly, you should be able to lead from any position. You might not have an official title, or be the boss of the company, but that does not restrict you from being able to step up and lead when a leader is needed. Taking a difficult task on or improving your workplace is a quick way to be noticed by your employer. Show that you have some gumption. One day it will be time for your supervisor to move on from their position, and you will most likely be the first person that comes to mind to replace them. You do not need to be formally in charge to step up and take charge when change is needed.

We have already discussed in this book how being an expert at some skill helps you to be a more emotionally intelligent person, but you should also know that it's okay that you don't know everything, just try to make sure that you know something. Let's assume you are performing really well at what it is you already do. That is great! But, you should try to learn new skills that apply to the new things your job demands. Do not simply lean back and accept that, " it's not my job, I'm not going to do it." Go above and beyond your skills, even in everyday life, not only the workplace.

As a leader, you need to be open and accepting of criticism. One trait that EVERYONE hates in a leader is not being able to accept that sometimes they are wrong. They absolutely refuse to admit that they are wrong, and often end up blaming someone else. Use this criticism to become a better person. Use it to grow as a leader. No leader is going to be absolutely perfect in the beginning, and receiving criticism should flatter you. When your followers feel comfortable enough talking with you to give you criticism, you know that you have done a good job communicating.

Use every opportunity you can get your hands on to communicate with your team and ask them what they need. You should be able to demonstrate that you understand what is required of you as the leader of your team, and that you understand the limits of your team. Always strive to improve the quality and efficiency of their work, but avoid becoming overbearing. All that is needed sometimes is a meeting in the very beginning of the work day with a sort of open mic feel to it. Let the team express what they want out of this project and what they need to do their best work, and if reasonable, provide that type of environment for them.

This leads us to communication skills. Good leaders are able to effectively and clearly communicate with their teams. This includes properly formatting emails, and writing and speaking professionally. Be consistent in the things you say, and do not stretch the truth for any reason. You should be honest with your team, because you would expect them to be honest with you. Avoid becoming emotionally with them and keep your tone appropriate. It is encouraging to your team to have a sour attitude when you have one first. They are a mirror reflection of what you are projecting to them.

Also, remove your desires from the actions you take for the team. Being a good leader requires making sacrifices, and the best thing for the team may not be the best thing for you. Loyalty is a rare trait, and it shows great character. In the business setting, loyalty is as important as showing up for work. Do not make any recommendations that are in conflict with what is happening, and give the credit for the finished project to your team, not yourself. When your team begins to trust that your motives are good for everyone and not just yourself, they begin to like and trust you.

Encourage creativity within your team. Letting your team know that they can express themselves allows them to feel comfortable doing their best work. They should be given enough slack to feel comfortable while working in the team, because feeling uncomfortable is going to make things a lot worse for everyone. Intellectually stimulate your team members and encourage them to think. Ask questions and expect answers. Offering a challenge to your group will offer the stimulation they need to feel comfortable and interested, and a challenging task keeps it fun.

Overall, be a passionate and expressive role model to your team. You should present a version of yourself that is the type of leader your team members want to be. Be model for the qualities you want to see in your teammates. You'll find that they will be more ept to begin mirroring your actions. After all, your followers are a reflection of who you are, and that is a big responsibility! Show them what the model looks like and they'll go for it. Hold that type of integrity close, because it is valuable and smart to have.

Chapter 15: Beginning to Practice Empathy

Empathy is putting yourself in the place of others. Emotionally intelligent people use the awareness of their emotions to first stop toxic behaviors and consider how the others feel. You can always improve your empathy. Empathy helps heal relationships and create new ones. Being a sensitive person does not make you weak or some type of secondhand person. It gives you insight to other people's feelings and increases your awareness of the emotional ambiance around you. Here are some ways you can learn to better practice empathizing and grow as an emotionally intelligent person.

Studies show that empathy is only partially an innate behavior, and it is partially learned. Taking on challenges and learning your limits may help humble you. Humility allows you to more easily feel what people are feeling when they feel like a failure, and humility erases cockiness and annoying behaviors you might have once had. By keeping active and avoiding reclusive behaviors, you will be positioned around emotions more frequently which opens a window to opportunity. The emotional growth you gain from doing new things and pushing yourself is worth the frustration.

Get out of the house. Go live your life a little. You should definitely try stepping out from your comfort zone. Seeing the world and other cultures help you to better appreciate them. It helps you to better appreciate diversity. Empathy comes from appreciating someone else's feelings, and being able to understand why they feel the way they do. Their experience in life was probably different than yours, and they may have learned to react differently to that type of situation than you did. We all need to collectively understand that we all feel differently, and we are entitled to our feelings.

Ask your friends and family what they think of your empathy skills. Ask them to answer honestly and let you know if you have been too soft or too harsh in the past. Remember, we are not afraid of criticism here, and we will take it humbly. Criticism is nothing more than opportunity to improve. Specifically, ask your peers what they think of your relationship skills. If they let you know you could improve on something, then make an effort to improve and ask them again periodically if they can see a difference. Bettering yourself should never be embarrassing, it should be a comfortable and positive experience.

Listen to what your heart is telling you and not so much your head. You might be quick to judge when you see someone crying over an experience you feel you could have personally handled well, but for all you know, they could have just went through much more than you are seeing. Maybe they also recently lost their job or went through a bad break up. Do not judge your books by the cover, instead put yourself in their place. Think about how they are feeling more than what you think of them in that moment. When your brain tells you to leave it for someone else to deal with, hopefully your heart is asking you to take a little time from your day to comfort that person who is in need of your help. You could very well save their life.

When speaking with others about their problems, ask them what it's like in their situation. Try to see things from their perspective so that you can get all of the details before you start creating assumptions. Ask them how they are perceiving you, and listen. They should feel comfortable opening up to you about these things, so if they feel uncomfortable, don't push it too far. Everything they disclose should be in confidence and consent. When you finally see things from their side, you may be surprised how similar their situation may feel to something you have experienced. Knowing their situation better will help you help them.

Maybe you should also take a moment to examine your biases. Everyone has things that lead them to think or react in certain ways, but it helps us to become more emotionally aware of ourselves when we can catch ourselves in the act and instead say no. It is best for the emotionally intelligent person to make choices based on all of the information they have and ignore the biases we know we have. This leads to better decision making and a more fair outlook. It doesn't make you a bad person for having biases, as many of them come from influences you first noticed when you were very young, but it makes you a better person to be able to set them aside for the sake of rationality.

Empathy also works best when you are being a good listener. Listening to someone makes them feel more comfortable trusting you with their concerns, and it makes them feel important. You will also learn from them. Some of us only listen half as much as we speak, but take the time to simply be quiet. Becoming a more empathetic listener involves giving the conversation your undivided attention, giving the speaker plenty of chances to let it all out and say what they need to say, asking insightful questions, and summarizing what you heard after they have finished talking.

Once you find yourself better able to empathize with your peers, you will find yourself becoming more aware of your own biases and emotions, and becoming a much better listener. Listening skills help you as a leader, because they make your followers more interested in voicing their opinions and concerns to you. A good leader should be open ears to any changes that need to be made or suggestions that need to be heard. Putting yourself in their shoes shows them that you are also wise, and in the long run, the trust you build is priceless.

Chapter 16: How Emotional Intelligence Affects your Motivation

Emotional intelligence positively boosts your ability to self-motivate, which leads to living a better life and more easily growing your career. The self-awareness and emotional capabilities of people who have a high EQ really shines a positive ray of sunshine on their motivation skills. Sometimes when we have had little motivation for a long tie, it is difficult to get motivated again, sort of like taking a cheat day that turns into a cheat week. We are simply humans, so this is natural to us. We want more than we can easily obtain, but we do not feel the motivation to try as hard as it takes to get what we want. The traits of an emotionally intelligent person which labels them as a self-motivator and go getter can be found within this chapter. Keep reading and ask yourself if you feel any of these traits describe you.

Motivated people set goals, and whenever they find themselves caught in a slump, they as themselves why that is. Maybe the things going on in your life right now are making you way too busy to even think about being positive. Or maybe you aren't getting enough sleep. Either way, you can get out of that slump. Setting a goal and meeting it is awesome, trust me. Goals help us concentrate our focus on the more important things, like the end goal. It is also easier to know for sure what it is you want when you are focusing on a single goal. Freelance motivation is pretty difficult, so make it easier by becoming a goal setter and a go getter!

Motivated people also look for inspiration. One of the biggest drives for anyone is something that truly inspires them in their core. Look for someone who might be a good role model or idol, and listen to the words they say. You can often easily find motivational speeches and inspiring stories on video streaming services. Emotional intelligence helps us to become inspired because people with higher EQs are deeper thinkers. They can appreciate the beauty in things that others might not always see. You can find inspiration anywhere if you look for it and genuinely hope to find it. It is an extremely positive trait to have to be able to spot inspiration from wherever you are.

Be excited to reach your goal. Do your best to feel and show enthusiasm. If someone is telling you they aren't feeling it or they no longer have faith in the process, tell them to keep moving forward, and be hopeful. As has already been mentioned, finding your inspiration can be the drive inside of you that makes you excited to wake up every morning and turn on the coffee machine, Excitement is a powerful emotion that causes us to do things we never thought humanly possible, because it gets our blood pumping and our adrenaline running through our bodies.

Anticipate the outcome. This might sound difficult, and many people brush it off as if it doesn't really matter. But it really works. It helps people who struggle with a nicotine addiction quit smoking after many tries. It helps people cut the alcohol out of their lives. Building anticipation for the outcome is done by thinking about what it will finally be like after you win.. If you find inspiration and wish to begin working towards one of you goals, do not begin right away. Many of us will get excited and in a rush and want to start as soon as we can. That can be the end of it all, though. Set a date in the future and make that your Start Date. Mark your calendar appropriately. Build excitement about that date, then make it seem as if it is the most important date of the month. In the meantime, start writing out a plan. You will see for yourself, by delaying your start, you are building anticipation and increasing your focus and energy for your goal.

Make your goal obtainable and remind yourself everyday. Maybe write it on a post-it note and stick it on the fridge, or you could write it on a whiteboard. Either way, you should try your best to remind yourself of your goal every day. It could even benefit you to post your goal online on social media so your peers can help you hold yourself accountable. If you were trying to lose weight, maybe create a chart of your weightloss and put it on your bathroom door. As long as Think about your goal everyday and ask for support. Maybe talking about your goal will help you obtain it. You can always find someone who will support you, even on social media. Reaching a new goal can be frightening and difficult, but when other people are sharing the experience with you, you might find that it's not that bad. Support networks keep the dream alive when you know longer feel like you can do it by yourself, and that is the only reason you need to reach out and ask for a little help staying motivated.you can visually see or hear your goal everyday,you will be more likely to reach it.

Understand that motivation is not a constant flow of easy peasy self-support. There may be periods where you find your motivation is shallow. It comes and it goes. This is one reason why self-motivation is so important for you to be able to achieve. When you feel tired of your goals, or just simply weak and exhausted, there won't always be someone next to you with a bottle of water telling you to get back in there. You have to be able to step up to the plate and swing by yourself sometimes. It's okay to get tired and it's okay to want to quit, but it is not okay to let those feelings pull your feet into the ground. The motivation isn't going to make you feel like sunshine and rainbows the entire time, it just helps get you started. You have to push yourself and show character once it starts to get difficult.

Stick with it and never give up. If you have to stop, make sure you are stopping because you have to, not because you chose to. Those are your goals. Those are your dreams. Stick to them hard, because life on this Earth is short, and you may not get another chance as good as the one you've got. Do not let yourself get deterred. You may not feel motivated today, and you may have to force yourself up and onto your feet, but you better grit your teeth and stick to it. The motivation will come back. It may come back a week or a month later, but it will come back. Your goal is a journey that is miles long, and this little spot where you don't feel as motivated is just a speed bump in the road. You have got to ride this road out like a wave across the ocean, dealing with all the ups and downs. Only after you find yourself climbing the hill, you will finally see how rewarding it is to get to go back down it.

Now since we have talked about all of this emotion and the tidal wave that it can be. Discouragement might come from your goals being set too big at first. It would be like saying, " my goal is to be a Doctor." without first starting with, " I want to obtain my bachelor's degree." Start with smaller goals and meet each one individually. This way, you have a plan. Do not, however, allow yourself to become lazy and use your smaller goals as an excuse to work easier. You do not have to start out by doing super intense workouts every day of the week, you can simply start small, and work your way up to doing what is comfortable for you, but again, do not allow these smaller goals to be your excuse to refrain from pushing yourself.

Once you begin to build on these small successes, you will learn how rewarding they are. You can't really fail if you start somewhere easy enough for you to surely succeed. Once you master that goal, reach for the next one, and then the next one, and then keep running after them. After a while, you will be able to look back on everything you have done and see how far it has gotten you. Do not forget to also share your successes with others. All of these positive things will help you learn to self motivate. Not to mention, by taking small steps, you are far less likely to fail.

Now here is a little time to take a break and read about your goals. Look at the finished product often, because this is going to motivate you. Remind yourself to keep looking at it and never forget why you started here. You started here because of that goal, so take a long look at it reach for it as hard as you can.

Also, maybe join an online forum or a social media group so you may surround yourself with people who share similar goals to you. These people are the ones who are going to help you get over those bumps in the road. Thank them for that. You are going to need an amazing support group, and those kinds of people more than likely have plenty of experience where you are lacking. Let them know that you are near to or far from your goal and remember to ask for help. They may tell you things you can not hear anywhere else, and they may have that vital tip you never knew that is an absolute game changer.

So no you are nearing the point of reaching your goal. Try your best to not stop and focus on the difficulties, focus on the reward you have coming for you in the end. There is more to life than the things that we find difficult to overcome, but those rare rewards in the end that are the kind of rewards that let us reflect on our hard work, those are precious. That is a precious piece of life that you should never let anyone take from you. When you put in the hard work, you can really do anything. You should aim high and work hard, because one day, you'll wake up and be a better you.

Last thing, do not let the negative thoughts outweigh the positive because of lack of character. This isn't easy for anyone, and no matter how the others made it look, do not be fooled by the very selective parts of the process you were shown. Everyone struggles with something, and everyone who has obtained your goal probably worked their fingertips off for it. Replace your negative thoughts with those, and watch your motivation take off. There is no such thing as negativity when you can shed light on any situation, because even a failure can be considered an opportunity to learn.

Chapter 17: Stress management the Intelligent Way

Managing stress in a healthy way is a part of building your emotional intelligence. Stress management is important for your mental and emotional health, because it provides an outlet for the negative feelings you have gathered throughout your day/week/year. This is why people often say, "I need a vacation!" You really do NEED a break from time to time, because life is stressful for everyone. Working long periods of time without a break is a straight shot to grumpiness, or worse, depression. Also, don't let anyone tell you that you take too many breaks or too much vacation. We are only on this earth one time, so make your life the best version it can be and ENJOY living. Let's talk about stress management.

First things first, you should avoid things that amplify your stress like nicotine, caffeine, and excessive alcohol. Coffee in the morning isn't a bad idea, but drinking it in excess can lead to fatigue later in the day accompanying a hard caffeine crash. Those are the worst. Maybe try eating a healthier breakfast with things in it that give you energy like eggs, milk, fruits, or granola.

As for the alcohol, there's nothing wrong with using alcohol as a tool for relaxing, but in excess, we all know what comes next. Hangovers. Hangovers make you feel super fatigued and very stressed, often coming with throwing up and headaches. Maybe opt for a glass of wine or a couple of beers instead of mixed spirits.

Avoid nicotine altogether if you can, because it has been scientifically proven that the nicotine is not what you crave, rather th

an the action of smoking or

chewing. We figure out that smoking= a smoke break, and we enjoy the time outside relaxing by sucking and exhaling, but the truth is, nicotine gives you headaches and drains your energy. Not to forget that tobacco products often lead to health problems as serious as fatal cases of cancer.

Second, you could try relieving some stress in a way that benefits your body physically, too! Yes, I am talking about exercise. Exercise isn't so bad if you really think about it, because you can always just go your own pace, and you don't even need equipment. You can find workout videos online very easily, and most of them do not require that you own anything super special. Try going for a walk, doing some squats, jumping jacks, or pushups, anything that you can do using your own body. Many people find that sport type exercising like boxing or shooting hoops is one of the best ways to deal with stress specifically related to anger. Letting out some energy while thinking about your stress is a great way to purge it from your mind.

Thirdly, try to get some decent sleep. Not everyone gets to sleep all night, sure, but you need to make time for yourself to get a reasonable amount of rest. Going too long without sleeping leads to serious fatigue and even sickness. It might be tempting to stay up late because you feel like the night time is your only free time, but if that truly is the case, you need to seriously adjust your schedule so you are taking more breaks in life. Money and bills are a part of being an adult, and they are very important, but living your life to pay bills and die is not ideal for anyone. So put that phone down, turn off the TV, and get some good sleep!

Now that you have exercised, slept, and adjusted your diet, maybe try a relaxation technique you haven't ever tried before, like yoga, baking, art, or drinking hot tea on the back porch. There are many things you probably haven't tried, like self-hypnosis or meditation. You could think of a self-calming mantra like, " Everything will be fine." or, " A bad day i not a bad life." Maybe it is time you dug that old instrument you haven't played in years out of the closet and blow off some dust. No need to be afraid of new things, just dip your foot in the water and see if you like it!

Also, try talking about your feelings with someone you trust. Throughout this book, I have talked about how important interacting with others about your feelings is important. It allows you to vent and shed your mind of any anger or negative feelings. Being stressed can influence things like judgement and attitude, an as long as you are interacting with others, they will be able to tell something is wrong with you. Ask them their opinions on the matters that stress you out, and let them tell you how they think you should handle it. You may not take their advice, but you should at least be open to it.

Have you ever tried keeping a journal? Writing down what stresses you out, and writing about your problems helps you cool down from a hard day. The cool thing about journals is that they don't tell your secrets, so you can write down whatever you want. You could write about someone who gives you a headache, or you could write down what you wish you could say to them. This is similar to writing an angry letter and throwing it away. Journals are very therapeutic, and they provide relief from having to keep your mouth shut and your thoughts to yourself. They are a window to expression, and you can get really creative with them. You could draw you stress instead of writing, music lyrics or poetry.

Try to take control of the problems that are causing you to stress out. If you can identify the culprit, squash it. Sometimes we forget that we are in charge of our own lives and it becomes easy to react to your problems without thinking. It also becomes easier to feel helpless in our own lives, but we are never hopeless. You can always reach out for help, but you must make that first action yourself. You have to be the first person to recognize the problem and decide that you want to do something about it. It is extremely difficult to help someone who does not want help.

Stress management is not a difficult thing to balance. All you need to remember to do is take breaks when you feel like you need one and ask for help if you need it. Of course, a healthy diet free of drugs and alcohol always helps, too. Most importantly, you need to know that needing a little stress management every once in awhile

Chapter 18: The Interpersonal Emotional Quotient

Unlike your intelligence quotient, or IQ, you Emotional Quotient measures your emotional intelligence rather than your general intelligence. Your EQ measure how well you think, understand your own emotions, and how well you can apply your emotions to real life.

Your emotional Quotient helps you to interact with people around you, and has been studied all over the world. Like we talked about in a previous chapter, your emotional quotient is directly tied to how well you perform in business and school environments. John D. Meyer is said to be one of the first people to really recognize and give emotional intelligence and your emotional quotient consideration.

One of the top reads on the emotional quotient is a book that was originally written in 1995 by Daniel Goleman. It is quite literally called *Emotional Intelligence.* This book was considered a best-seller and brought nw insight to the EQ that people had never heard of before. For many, the Emotional Quotient was a new concept, because it was not taught in schools. It put the brain and the concept of intelligence in a new light, because it was no longer about simple, abstract thinking, but it now involved understanding emotions and being able to be measured based on the ability to interact in social situations.

The interpersonal aspects of the emotional quotient can be described as the things you do and think about in order to relate with other people. These interpersonal skills involve communicating, conflict management, rational thinking, problem solving, and more.

Chapter 19: The Intrapersonal Aspects

Emotional intelligence also has parts of it that we call "intrapersonal". Intrapersonal parts are the ones that occur within one's own mind. People who have strong intrapersonal intelligence are often very aware of themselves and their surroundings. They are good problem solvers and communicators because they often think about their words and actions before expressing them. One of the biggest things that set our human conscience aside from other animals sis our ability to think in full sentences and entire languages to ourselves. We are taught to think before we speak from an early age, but we are not often taught how special that truly is. It is a sign of a very emotionally intelligent person to consciously take consideration of their words.

There have been studies which resulted in theories suggesting that humans evolved to talk to themselves to avoid silence. Naturally, human beings crave noise of some kind. Elongated episodes of silence can be "creepy" and cause us to feel uncomfortable. Silence is actually a semi-common phobia. As long as we can not hear sound, we are on alert and quickly become hyper sensitive to any movements, smells, or sounds. Becoming silent and freezing is a sign of fear, so scientists have guessed that it was a way that early humans communicated to each other that there was danger nearby.

Although not everyone is naturally in tune with their intrapersonal mind, these skills can be taught. Intrapersonal skills help you know what things you excel in and what things you are limited by. Intrapersonal skills are especially helpful in assisting you when dealing with conflict, managing stress, and handling time.

Chapter 20: A Healthy Mood

Emotional intelligence is best absorbed when your mood is healthy and positive. Not everyone floats out of bed in the morning like an angel and is happy to wake up. Having a positive attitude can be a challenge some day whens you are lacking on sleep or hungry. It can be a challenge to refrain from acting out or sighing and rolling your eyes over small things when you are in a bad mood. By exploring the ways your mood can change and how to control your feelings, you can improve your life and the responses you give to negative stimuli.

First, you need to understand what sorts of things are influencing your mood. Sometimes you become grouchy when you are lacking an important part of a balanced diet, like being dehydrated. Food can also be the main thing that stresses you out. Eating disorders sometime cause us to become stressed out after eating things like sweets or carbs. Certain disorders even lead us to feel like we need to punish ourselves for eating. Though, not eating foods you enjoy can also lead one to become stressed, like taking a break from eating things you used to eat daily like sweets, sodas, or alcohol.

Obviously, stress will affect your mood as well. Stress causes feelings of fatigue and disinterest in daily activities you would usually enjoy. You mood can quickly become depressed if you allow stress to take over. Lack of sleep, or sometimes in rare cases, too much sleep also causes you to feel like you are being dragged down emotionally. This feeling almost always accompanies the urge to stay in bed and sleep more, even when you are not feeling physically tired. It may also cause headaches or mood swings where your attitude changes quickly and without warning by a small trigger.

Boosting your mood and controlling your attitude can be down safely and naturally. There is no need for medicine if you are not very deeply scarred or depressed. You may want to speak to your doctor or psychiatrist first, but trying natural and healthy ways should be the first step towards improving the way you feel. Here are some of those ways.

Not blaming yourself is one step to take. Your attitude might be the product of an event in your life that was not enjoyable, but blaming yourself for what happened is not the best route to overcoming it. It is a simple thing you can do to overcome depression and anger. Tell yourself that there was nothing you could do, or that you are confident that you did enough. You should avoid allowing yourself to feel guilty or inadequate, because you are worth more than that. Feeling happy should never feel like it is a privilege. You should always feel confident enough to remind yourself that it is a right.

Look at things from the bright side. Your mood is not going to stick around forever, because you have control over your own thoughts and feelings. This is where self-awareness comes into play. You can choose to see the brighter side of things, and you can choose to refuse to sit in your own pity and get up and do something about it. If there is not a brighter side that you can think of or visualize, always remember that your ability to control your emotions and attitude is a bright side in itself. See the light in the darkness.

Get sleep and close your eyes for the night. When it comes to bed time, this is something to avoid skipping out on. Put your phone down so that you aren't staring at a screen. Staring at bright screens right before going to sleep causes your sleep to have worse quality. You should try your best to sleep with the lights off and no sounds in the background, but if it helps you to stay asleep, listening to calm ocean sounds or white noises is a good idea. Another thing to do is make sure to wake up at a decent time every day. Maybe draw back the curtains and let some sn fill your room. You do not have to be a morning person, but you should make a good effort to get out of bed on the FIRST alarm.

The ambience of a room also greatly influences the way you feel. Sitting in a dark room by yourself is not the best way to promote a positive attitude. Try walking in the garden ir decorating a little. Surround yourself with people you enjoy being around if it is possible. It had been proven that these things assist your mood. Bright and open spaces are the best, especially if the light is coming from natural lighting.

Animals are another tool for boosting your mood. Animals can be so darn cute, and you can always find plenty of photos and videos of puppies and kittens on the internet anytime. Petting a pet can be very therapeutic and has been proven to reduce stress levels. Studies from accredited research universities have found that in only 15 minutes, petting your dog can cause your brain to release feel good chemicals like serotonin and oxytocin. Their soft fur and warm bellies always bring a smile to people's faces. If you have a pet, maybe trying to dedicate more time out of your day to pet it and love it will lead you to a significant mood boost.

Here is an interesting study to consider. A study conducted by Clark University was conducted by asking the participant to smile, and the other half to frown. They did not truly feel the emotions that traditionally lead to those emotions, but they were specifically instructed to force those expressions. After an amount of time, both groups were shown the same cartoons. Unsurprisingly, the group who was instructed to force themselves to smile ended up all rating the cartons funnier than the ones who had to frown. Perhaps the takeaway from this study was that by making yourself smile, and in a sense, "faking it until you're making it", you could improve the status of your mood and attitude by simply tricking your brain into thinking you are happy.

If you are a woman and you have noticed a decline in the positivity of you workdays or frequent mood swings, you might need to consider a different form of birth control methods. Taking the pill has been known to cause mood swings and depression in some women, and maybe a different method is all you need to help you feel better. In some cases, it could simply be the hormones in the birth control and you should opt for non-hormonal methods like condoms or abstinence. It has been the opinion of doctors that problems with one hormonal method is foreshadowing problems with other methods.

Now, consider getting creative. Artistic expression is one of the oldest methods of stress relief and can also change your mood. Art simply takes your mind off of things and helps you relax. There is no need for drama when you are too busy thinking about the unique piece of art that you are creating. Some artists even express their negative feelings through their art, and by doing so, they find it is easier to share their feelings with other people. Art is like a metaphor for your feelings, and if something as simple as a little doodling in your notepad is going to make you feel better, I say go for it.

Chapter 21: Strategies of Success

Being successful mean that you achieved your goals. You set out for something greater than yourself and you seized it. Successful can even be described as a social status. Anyone can be successful, and achieving success takes a plan. There are a few resources out there that claim to hand you success in a wrapped gift box, but the raw truth of it is that it takes time and hard work. With dedication and effort, you will be able to obtain your goals n no time. Here are a couple of strategies that can help you along the journey.

First things first, take risks. Success is limited, and it isn't going to show up in your backyard. Success presents itself to the people who wake up early and decide to be a go-getter. You won't gain anything from staying at home, so talk yourself into taking some risk. Risk can be small or large. Risk might involve taking out a loan to start your business, or uploading you art to sell. It might be an investment or a bet, but in any form it is still a risk, so tread cautiously, but be brave. Never put yourself in a situation where the risk you took was bigger than something you can come out of.

Do your best to surround yourself with people you consider to be successful. You are never too old to learn from someone and it is best that it be people you know. By observing them, you might pick up a couple of habits of a successful person, or even some pro tips. Ask them what they think of your plan for success and consider what they say to be helping you, even if it seems negative or disbelieving.

Have a plan, but be spontaneous. You simply can not live your entire life being ruled by things like others' opinions of you and money. Money helps us to live. It even helps us live comfortably, but it is not the god of our lives. Knowing the steps you plan on taking before taking them is helpful obviously because it takes out a large percentage that you will be surprised with a rude awakening, but also, if you feel like risking your savings, assess how bad it truly is. Spending a little money on yourself because you happened to come up on a sale at your favorite store, or buying yourself a muffin instead of an apple is not the end of the world. Do what makes you happy.

Speaking of being happy, you should feel confident in yourself. It is easy to lose confidence when the going gets tough, but with a little self motivation, you can convince yourself to stay inspired and work as hard as you need to. Visualize the reward you will get from this.

Next, you should always strive to be learning something. Learn to relax or maybe learn how to work smarter. Be open to criticism and make yourself the person you always knew you could be. Strive to maybe teach yourself as well. Maybe search for some resources online and read up about other successful people.

Successful people come in all shapes and sizes. Do not give up, you are going to get there. It may take a little time, but you are NOT in a race, so put your big boy britches on and get to work. By having a solid plan, setting some goals, relaxing every once in awhile, and letting yourself eat a muffin is a solid strategy to reach those goals.

Conclusion

Emotional intelligence is the guide to becoming a good friend, and a good fellow human being. It can be instructional, informative, and inspirational because it is all within you. Everyone has some level of emotional intelligence, though it may not be the same, and it can be taught. As young children, we wonder what being an adult is like. We think that being an adult is being able to express your emotions however you want because they see the way adults speak to them with no reprecussions.

Life is not easy for anyone, yet it is interesting that human beings strive to make it look that way. We live in a pay per view world now, and speed and convenience are the two most important things to being young. Even though this is true, there is still a little bit of positivity in the world. We can hope for a bright future… a future where our children are taught to experience emotions and become aware of themselves. We could live in a wor;d with no communication barriers one day.

Emotional intelligence is unique and important because it sparks our curiosity. This is what makes us human. We are human because we are beautiful in our uniquely different ways, and we are lucky enough to be highly evolved enough to see that. I hope you found this practical guide informative and eye opening. It is a journey to self-discovery and it takes time, but by learning who your are inside of your own mind and feeling you emotions the way they aremeant to be felt, you can grow into the person you looked up to as a child. Good luck with your journey!

Sources...

2011-2019, (. C. (n.d.). Dealing with Stress - Ten Tips. Retrieved from https://www.skillsyouneed.com/ps/stress-tips.html

5 Actionable Tips to Develop Empathy and Become a More Empathetic Person. (2017, June 14). Retrieved from https://mindmaven.com/blog/5-tips-to-become-more-empathetic/

7 tips for dealing with change. (n.d.). Retrieved from https://au.reachout.com/articles/7-tips-for-dealing-with-change

9 Ways to Give Effective Employee Feedback. (2018, May 03). Retrieved from https://www.15five.com/blog/9-ways-to-give-effective-employee-feedback/

14 Essential Tips for Meeting a Deadline. (n.d.). Retrieved from

20 Tips to Help You Act Like a Professional in the Workplace. (2016, March 09). Retrieved from https://www.decadirect.org/2016/03/09/20-tips-to-help-you-act-like-a-professional-in-the-workplace/

Bradberry, T. (2014, October 08). The Most And Least Emotionally Aware Countries. Retrieved from https://www.forbes.com/sites/travisbradberry/2013/08/17/the-most-and-least-emotionally-aware-countries/#21ec6ccd3596

Brown, L. (2019, March 26). How to find meaning in life (it's easier than you think). Retrieved from https://hackspirit.com/how-to-find-meaning-in-life-its-easier-than-you-think/

https://business.tutsplus.com/articles/14-essential-tips-for-meeting-a-deadline--fsw-240

Culture Influences Brain Function, Study Shows. (2008, January 13). Retrieved from https://www.sciencedaily.com/releases/2008/01/080111102934.htm \

Does culture affect our personality? - Individual Traits and Culture. (n.d.). Retrieved from https://explorable.com/culture-and-personality

Edberg, H. (2019, March 04). How to Overcome Failure: 9 Powerful Habits. Retrieved from https://www.positivityblog.com/how-to-overcome-failure/

Deutschendorf, H., & Deutschendorf, H. (2015, June 22). Why Emotionally Intelligent People Are More Successful. Retrieved from https://www.fastcompany.com/3047455/why-emotionally-intelligent-people-are-more-successful

Harvard Health Publishing. (n.d.). 12 ways to keep your brain young. Retrieved from https://www.health.harvard.edu/mind-and-mood/12-ways-to-keep-your-brain-young

How Do Emotions Work? (n.d.). Retrieved from https://kids.frontiersin.org/article/10.3389/frym.2017.00069

Lewis, T. (2018, September 28). Human Brain: Facts, Functions & Anatomy. Retrieved from https://www.livescience.com/29365-human-brain.html

Lsweatt Https://www.success.com/author/lsweatt/. (-0001, November 30). Do These 7 Things If You Want to Become a Leader. Retrieved from https://www.success.com/do-these-7-things-if-you-want-to-become-a-leader/

National Institute on Drug Abuse. (n.d.). What are marijuana's long-term effects on the brain? Retrieved from https://www.drugabuse.gov/publications/research-reports/marijuana/what-are-marijuanas-long-term-effects-brain

(n.d.). Retrieved from https://facilethings.com/blog/en/lizard-brain

Sandford, K. (2019, February 18). Adapting to Change: Why It Matters and How to Do It. Retrieved from https://www.lifehack.org/372463/why-you-need-adapt-change
Reptilian Brain of Survival and Mammalian Brain. (n.d.). Retrieved from https://www.gracepointwellness.org/109-post-traumatic-stress-disorder/article/55760-reptilian-brain-of-survival-and-mammalian-brain

Thompson, V. (2018, June 13). A pair of neuroscientists finds that investigating emotions is easier done than said. Retrieved from https://blogs.sciencemag.org/books/2018/06/18/the-neuroscience-of-emotion/

Three Recent Studies on Emotional Intelligence (EI). (n.d.). Retrieved from https://www.psychologytoday.com/us/blog/here-there-and-everywhere/201111/three-recent-studies-emotional-intelligence-ei

Bradberry, Travis and Greaves, Jean. (2009). Emotional Intelligence 2.0. San Francisco: Publishers Group West. ISBN 978-0-9743206-2-5

Petrides, K.V.; Pita, R.; Kokkinaki, F. (2007). "The location of trait emotional intelligence in personality factor space". British Journal of Psychology. 98 (2): 273–289.

Petrides, K.V.; Furnham, A. (2001). "Trait emotional intelligence: Psychometric investigation with reference to established trait taxonomies". European Journal of Personality. 15 (6): 425–448.

Pérez, J.C., Petrides, K.V., & Furnham, A. (2005). Measuring trait emotional intelligence. In R.

Schulze and R.D. Roberts (Eds.), International Handbook of Emotional Intelligence (pp.181–201). Cambridge, Massachusetts: Hogrefe & Huber.

Petrides, K.V.; Furnham, A. (2003). "Trait emotional intelligence: behavioral validation in two studies of emotion recognition and reactivity to mood induction". European Journal of

Personality. 17: 39–75. Mikolajczak, Luminet; Leroy; Roy (2007). "Psychometric Properties of the Trait Emotional Intelligence Questionnaire: Factor Structure, Reliability, Construct, and

Incremental Validity in a French-Speaking Population". Journal of Personality Assessment

Vernon, P.A.; Petrides, K.V.; Bratko, D.; Schermer, J.A. (2008). "A behavioral genetic study of trait emotional intelligence". Emotion. 8

What Are Basic Emotions? (n.d.). Retrieved from https://www.psychologytoday.com/us/blog/hide-and-seek/201601/what-are-basic-emotions

What Is Self-Awareness? (and 8 Ways to Become More Self Aware). (2019, January 12). Retrieved from https://www.developgoodhabits.com/what-is-self-awarenYour Brain on Books:

10 Ways Reading Affects Psyche. (2016, March 31). Retrieved from https://oedb.org/ilibrarian/your-brain-on-books-10-things-that-happen-to-our-minds-when-we-read/ess/

Your Brain on Books: 10 Ways Reading Affects Psyche. (2016, March 31). Retrieved from https://oedb.org/ilibrarian/your-brain-on-books-10-things-that-happen-to-our-minds-when-we-read/

Zen habits : Breathe. (n.d.). Retrieved from https://zenhabits.net/get-off-your-butt-16-ways-to-get-motivated-when-youre-in-a-slump/

Schlinger, H. D. (2009). Some clarifications on the role of inner speech in consciousness. Consciousness and Cognition (18), 530-531.
^

Jones, S. R., & Fernyhoug, C. (2007). Thought as action: Inner speech, self-monitoring, and auditory verbal hallucinations. Consciousness and Cognition, 16, 391-399.

Seal, M. L., Aleman, A., & McGuire, P. K. (2004). Compelling imagery, unanticipated speech and deceptive memory: Neurocognitive models of auditory verbal hallucinations in schizophrenia. Cognitive Neuropsychiatry, 9, 43–72.

Macedonia, J. (1986). "Individuality in the contact call of the ring-tailed lemur (Lemur catta)". American Journal of Primatology, 11, 163-179

Jordania, J. (2009). "Times to Fight and Times to Relax: Singing and Humming at the Beginnings of Human Evolutionary History". Kadmos, 1, 272–277

Gammage, K. L., Hardy, J., & Hall, C. G. (2001). A description of self-talk in exercise. Psychology of Sport and Exercise, 2, 233–247

Zell, E., Warriner, A. B., & Albarracín, D. (2012). Splitting of the mind: When the You I talk to is Me and needs commands. Social Psychological and Personality Science, 3, 549–555

Oliver, E. J., Markland, D., Hardy, J., & Petherick, C. M. (2008). The effects of autonomy-supportive versus controlling environments on self-talk. Motivation & Emotion, 32, 200–212.

Dolcos, S. & Albarracin, D. (2014). The inner speech of behavioral regulation: Intentions and task performance strengthen when you talk to yourself as a You. European Journal of Social Psychology

Cunningham, Stanley B. (1992). "Intrapersonal Communication: A Review and Critique,"
JSTOR

Demetriou, A., Christou, C.; Spanoudis, G.; Platsidou, M. (2002). "The development of mental processing: Efficiency, working memory, and thinking". Monographs of the Society of Research in Child Development. 67 (268).

Demetriou, A.; Kazi, S. (2006). "Self-awareness in g (with processing efficiency and reasoning".

Intelligence. 34 (3): 297–317.

Steven Mithen 2005 edition|"Creativity in Human Evolution and Prehistory"

Rolf W. Frohlich 2009 edition|"Evolutionary Intelligence: The Anatomy of Human Survival"

"About Us | Johnson O'Connor Research Foundation". jocrf.org. Retrieved 7 May 2019.

"Aptitude Testing and Research since 1922 | Johnson O'Connor Research Foundation". www.jocrf.org. Retrieved 7 May 2019.